THE GREATEST GOLF COURSES

and how they are played

- -

NORTH AMERICA

Previous page: Emerald Reef Golf Club, Bahamas;
This page: Black Mesa Golf Club, New Mexico

General Editor: Mark Rowlinson

THE GREATEST GOLF COURSES
and how they are played

NORTH AMERICA

hamlyn

Contributors

This book features the greatest golf courses in North America that display architectural brilliance or are simply important in the history of the game. These golf courses were selected by an international panel of course designers, ex-Tour pros and leading golf journalists.

General Editor

Mark Rowlinson (UK) has been associated with *The World Atlas of Golf* since 1990, both editorially and as a contributor. He has also written *A Place to Golf* and *The Times Guide to the Golf Courses of Great Britain and Ireland*.

The panel

Tom Doak (US) is widely recognized as one of the world's finest golf-course architects, he has designed four courses currently ranked among *Golf Magazine*'s international top 100. Tom's unique body of historical and design knowledge has also been showcased in the classic *The Anatomy of a Golf Course* and *The Confidential Guide* and *The Life and Work of Dr Alister MacKenzie*.

Ran Morrissett (US) runs GolfClubAtlas.com, the world's premier golf architecture-related website. He is also a *Golf Magazine* ratings panelist who has resided in both the United States and Australia. A widely respected golf journalist, Ran's extensive travel and unique eye for great architecture give him an unsurpassed knowledge of the world's great courses and the intricacies of their design.

The 18th hole at Whistling Straits, Wisconsin

Daniel Wexler (US) is a California-based writer and former golf professional. He is one of America's leading golf historians, with a particular knowledge of classic course design. Daniel is the author of four books including *The Missing Links: America's Greatest Lost Golf Courses and Holes* and *The Book of Golfers: A Biographical History of the Royal & Ancient Game*.

Noel Freeman (US) works in the financial industry in New York City. He has travelled the globe in study of the greatest golf courses and the allure of finding a hidden gem.

Ben Cowan-Dewar (Canada) is the Chairman of GOLFTI, an internationally renowned tour operator. As well as sitting on the *Golf Magazine* panel that is the authoritative rating of the world's finest courses, Ben is a partner of the acclaimed golf architecture-related website GolfClubAtlas.com. He currently resides with his wife and son in Nova Scotia, Canada, where he is overseeing development of Cabot Links.

Banff Springs Golf Club, Canada

Contents

United States and Canada

The first mention of golf in America came in 1659 when the game was banned from the streets of Albany, New York. It is known that golf was played in the Carolinas from the mid-1740s, but golf as we know it today only became established in North America towards the end of the 19th century.

Unlike in Scotland, where the game has long been accessible to the masses, golf in North America began largely as a province of the wealthy, played almost exclusively at private clubs and resorts that, by virtue of catering solely to the affluent, were themselves essentially private.

Early resorts occasionally lay in remote locales, while private club development came almost entirely in the major population centres. The continent's first golf club (Royal Montreal) was

Golf course architect Donald Ross (left) and Richard S Tufts (3rd from left), future President of the USGA, at Pinehurst Resort, 1926.

established in 1873 in Canada's second largest city, and the majority of America's prominent early entries were situated in cities such as New York, Chicago, Boston, Philadelphia and San Francisco.

Course design was generally rudimentary, performed in what today would seem a remarkable hurry by all manner of Scottish émigrés who, to an audience of neophytes, surely appeared accomplished experts. Men such as Alex Findlay, Robert and James Foulis, and the prolific Tom Bendelow (who claimed to have completed more than 600 projects) were among the first to make golf architecture a primary source of income, often simply walking a property once, marking the locations of prospective tees and greens, then moving on in a design style pejoratively referred to by historians as 'eighteen stakes on a Sunday afternoon'.

THE GOLDEN AGE

Though courses such as Myopia Hunt Club and Garden City signalled the dawn of a more strategically interesting approach, it was Charles Blair Macdonald's 1911 National Golf Links of America that jump-started the process, lifting the continent's perception of what a golf course could be, and kicking off the glorious two-decade era known as North American golf design's Golden Age.

Ben Hogan hits an immaculate 1-iron to the final green at Merion in 1950 to tie the lead in the US Open. He went on to win the play off against Lloyd Mangrum and George Fazio.

The Golden Age is primarily recalled for its famous architects, which included visiting Britons (Willie Park Jnr, Harry Colt and Charles Alison), transplanted Britons (Donald Ross and Dr Alister MacKenzie) and North American natives (Charles Blair Macdonald, A.W. Tillinghast, Stanley Thompson, William Flynn and George Thomas). But far beyond these names, this was an era that saw North American design take a quantum leap forward in terms of both quantity and quality. Regarding the former, in the United States alone the total number of courses rocketed from fewer than 750 in 1916 to nearly 6,000 in 1930, as advanced earthmoving equipment allowed the reshaping of less-advantageous terrain and as modernized agronomical techniques opened up previously ill-suited hot-weather climates to sustainable turf growth. But it was the leap in quality that was most significant. Working in an era when more first-class sites remained available, and before myriad environmental issues limited their ability to reshape the land to their every

The famous Church Pews bunker separating the 3rd and 4th fairways at Oakmont Country Club.

whim, the designers of the Golden Age succeeded in producing a generation of strategic, aesthetically inviting facilities so fine that they have continued to dominate pretty well every prominent course ranking in the past 75 years.

Though a handful of significant courses were completed during the 1930s, in broad terms the Golden Age ended with the October 1929 crash of the American stock market. The economic ravages of the ensuing Depression, combined with the austerity of the Second World War, added up to a nearly two-decade hiatus in golf-course construction, an extended stagnancy that outlived the careers (and lives) of most Golden Age designers. When the industry's postwar recovery started during the 1950s, a new generation of architects was led by Robert

Trent Jones Snr, former apprentice to the great Canadian designer Stanley Thompson and a man whose self-proclaimed 'heroic' design style did much to transform the industry. Robert Trent Jones's primary national competition came from a William Flynn protégé, Dick Wilson, as well as Wilson's one-time partner Joe Lee, while men such as Geoffrey Cornish, Robert von Hagge, George Cobb, Clinton 'Robbie' Robinson and William Mitchell headed a long list who found great success on a more regional level.

THE MOVE TO SUBURBIA
With major urban areas no longer regularly offering sufficient developable land, golf construction moved out to the suburbs, as well as into the far wider destination resort market.

Largely at the impetus of Robert Trent Jones, courses became longer, and featured larger greens and the copious use of sand and water. It was, unfortunately, a design style that bequeathed little in the way of long-term greatness, with relatively few of that era's top new courses rating among the continent's best today.

A welcome turn back to more strategically interesting courses began in the late 1960s and early '70s, led primarily by Pete Dye, an ex-insurance salesman who, after a 1963 visit to Scotland, began to incorporate into his designs such Old World features as railway sleepers, unmanicured rough and pot bunkers. Even more importantly, Dye's most famous period courses typically measured under 6,800 yards and thus placed only the occasional emphasis on power – a significant shift from the Jones-inspired norm.

THE RISE OF RESORT COURSES

As travel became ever easier, post-1970s course development ranged even farther afield, frequently centring around resort areas such as Palm Springs or Myrtle Beach, or late-developing cities or regions such as Atlanta, Orlando and the American desert south-west. Pete Dye was joined by prominent competitors – Tom Fazio, Arthur Hills and Robert Trent Jones's sons Rees and Robert Jnr – but a major new factor in the marketplace was the 'player–architect', a big-name group of superb players led by Jack Nicklaus, with Arnold Palmer, Gary Player, Tom Weiskopf and, more recently, Greg Norman all following suit. In this era where an architect's name became a key marketing tool for developers, and where the frequent use of less-than-ideal sites mandated major earthmoving, overall project expenses rocketed – occasionally costing as much as US$20 million.

The new millennium has seen at least a partial rejection of such profligacy, with most of the continent's top new courses representing classically natural designs, built relatively inexpensively by men such as Bill Coore and Ben Crenshaw, Tom Doak and Gil Hanse. It has been a welcome trend both stylistically and economically. But with unchecked advances in playing equipment fuelling the demand for larger sites, located increasingly farther from major metropolitan markets, can the future of North American golf-course development remain a rosy one?

Bandon Trails was the third course constructed at Bandon Dunes Resort. There are now five courses.

North-eastern states

The early golfing crowd was largely an affluent one, generally residing in population centres such as New York, Philadelphia and Boston, and building courses both in their home neighbourhoods and at summer resort retreats such as Southampton and Newport. Given the prosperity of these golfers, the great majority of these courses were private. These Golden Age designs have also come to represent an especially high percentage of the north-east's total course inventory, because huge postwar suburban growth left little land for modern golf development. In fact, nowhere else in the United States does the balance, both in quality and quantity, so favour the old over the new.

GOLF AROUND NEW YORK

The New York metropolitan area was the north-east's first hotbed of golf, with well over 200 pre-Second World War courses springing up between northern Westchester County and the eastern tip of Long Island, most built (or rebuilt) by the great architects of the day. Westchester itself remains one of the nation's best provided golfing counties, led by a cluster of A. W. Tillinghast-designed parkland courses, which include one of the world's great 36-hole facilities at Winged Foot, its comparably ranked next-door neighbour Quaker Ridge[1], and a recently restored gem, Fenway[2]. Westchester also features two regular professional tournament sites, the 36-hole Walter Travis-designed Westchester Country Club[3] and Wykagyl[4]. It also has historically prominent venues: Apawamis[5], site of Harold Hilton's landmark 1911 US Amateur victory; Siwanoy[6], the home of the 1916's inaugural PGA Championship; Sleepy

Hollow[7]; Knollwood[8]; and, though rebuilt by Jack Nicklaus in 1985, St Andrew's[9].

Within New York City proper, golf is largely confined to under-maintained but occasionally interesting public courses. A prominent exception is Inwood[10], which lies across the marshes from Kennedy International Airport and was the site of Bobby Jones's first Major title, the 1923 US Open.

Long Island golf is generally associated with the links-like terrain of the Hamptons, where the National Golf Links of America, Shinnecock Hills and Maidstone lead the way. Elsewhere, the public 90-hole megacomplex at Bethpage State Park stands out, but Long Island is also noteworthy for its remarkable number of good-quality Golden Age layouts. Charles Blair Macdonald/Seth Raynor designs at The Creek[11] and Piping Rock[12] are significant, as is a long list of charmingly quirky facilities such as Engineers[13], Huntington[14], Fresh Meadow[15] and the Rockaway Hunting

Club[16], and such historic venues as Nassau[17] and Cherry Valley[18]. And Fishers Island represents a blue-chip asset on the Long Island ledger. A special place is reserved for Garden City Golf Club[19], arguably America's first truly great course, whose development owes much to the great amateur golfer Walter Travis, an Australian by birth but an immigrant to the United States.

GARDEN CITY GOLF CLUB

Travis took up the game in America and, despite starting aged 35, quickly found huge success, claiming three US Amateur titles between 1900 and 1903, then famously becoming the first foreigner to win the (British) Amateur Championship in 1904. He joined Garden City in 1899, two years after its foundation.

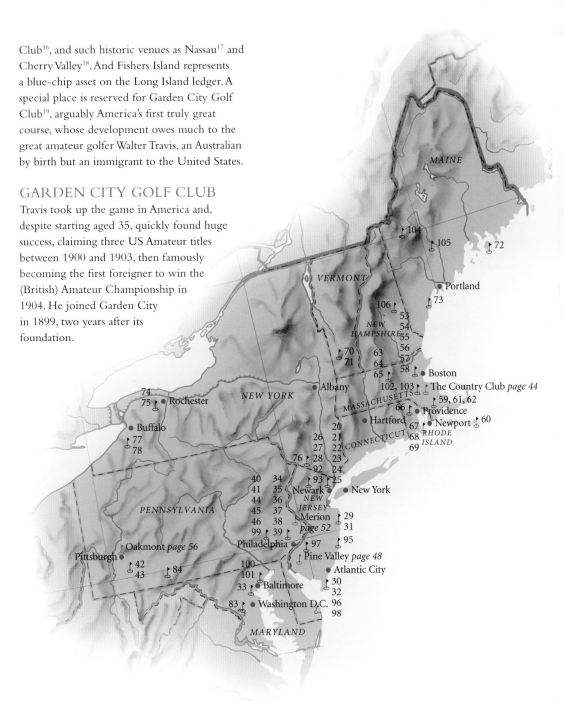

MAINE

104

105

72

VERMONT

Portland

106

53

73

NEW HAMPSHIRE

54

55

56

70

63

57

71

64

58

Boston

65

102, 103

The Country Club *page 44*

Albany

MASSACHUSETTS

59, 61, 62

74

66

Providence

75

Rochester

NEW YORK

Hartford

67

Newport

60

Buffalo

20

CONNECTICUT

68

RHODE

77

26

21

69

ISLAND

78

27

22

76

28

23

92

24

40

34

93

25

41

35

Newark

New York

44

36

NEW

45

37

JERSEY

29

46

38

Merion

31

99

39

page 52

95

Philadelphia

97

Oakmont *page 56*

100

Pine Valley *page 48*

Pittsburgh

101

42

Atlantic City

43

84

30

33

Baltimore

32

83

Washington D.C.

96

98

MARYLAND

PENNSYLVANIA

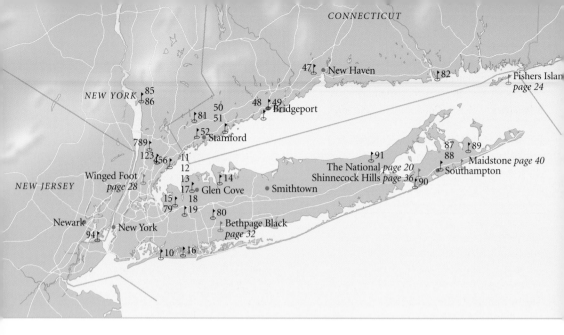

New Haven

Fishers Islan *page 24*

NEW YORK 85 86

50
81 51
48 49 Bridgeport

52 Stamford

789
123 56 11
12
13 14
17 Glen Cove
15 18
79 19 80
10 16

Winged Foot *page 28*

NEW JERSEY

Newark
94 New York

Bethpage Black *page 32*

Smithtown

The National *page 20*
Shinnecock Hills *page 36* 90

91

87 89
88
Maidstone *page 40*
Southampton

Garden City had opened as a Devereux Emmet-designed nine-holer known as the Island Links in 1897. The following year Emmet revised and extended this loop to 18 holes. In order to do this, he took a cue from the many Scottish courses he had visited: moving minimal earth, he created greens that were little more than natural extensions of each hole's fairway.

In 1906, Travis, an influential figure and regular critic of the game's rudimentary nature in America, provided Garden City with a list of proposed renovations that were quickly implemented. Central to these changes was his strong dislike of the many cross-bunkers that fronted Emmet's fairways. These were thus replaced by more than 50 new bunkers built alongside and at angles to many fairways, enhancing the course's strategic aspect considerably. Travis further added contour to a number of greens as well as the occasional perimeter mounding, which, though undeniably outlandish in spots, feels delightfully quaint today. His final renovative touch was the impressively deep bunkers.

NEW JERSEY GEMS

With its clubs sharing membership in the Metropolitan Golf Association, northern New Jersey enjoys a similar golfing history and demographic to New York, with classic courses – the majority private – dominating the landscape. Best-known are A. W. Tillinghast's 36 holes at Baltusrol[20] (the only club to host US Opens on both its courses), Tillinghast's charming Somerset Hills[21], and national tournament venues including Donald Ross's Plainfield[22], 36 holes at Montclair[23] and 27 fine Tillinghast holes at Ridgewood[24], host to the 1935 Ryder Cup. Former Seth Raynor partner Charles Banks's designs at Forsgate[25] and The Knoll[26], 36 much-altered holes at Canoe Brook[27], and Ross's Mountain Ridge[28] top a long list of honourable mentions.

Southern New Jersey is best known for Pine Valley, rated in many quarters as the game's finest course. But the region's golf history is rooted in early resort development along the Atlantic, where courses such as Hollywood[29], the 36-hole Seaview Resort[30],

Lakewood[31] and the recently modernized Atlantic City CC[32] have long entertained visitors. Farther south, Maryland offers a particularly fine entry – A.W. Tillinghast's East Course at the Baltimore CC[33].

PENNSYLVANIA COURSES

The Philadelphia area features an impressive classic course collection of its own, including famous Merion as well as Donald Ross's recently restored work at Aronimink[34]. Although in total Ross designed or renovated nearly a dozen Philadelphia-area courses, the architect most closely associated with the city is William Flynn, whose stable of first-class suburban courses is led by Huntingdon Valley[35], Manufacturers[36], Rolling Green[37] and the Philadelphia CC[38]. Like New York, Philadelphia's list of second-rank classics is a long one, and includes A.W. Tillinghast's Philadelphia Cricket Club[39] and Donald Ross's Gulph Mills[40], as well as Flynn and Willie Park Jnr designs at the 36-hole Philmont CC[41].

Oakmont and Seth Raynor's Fox Chapel[42] have long kept the Pittsburgh area on the golfing map. Elsewhere, Tillinghast's Sunnehanna[43] continues to host its nationally prominent amateur event, Herbert Strong's Old Course at Saucon Valley[44] has welcomed a US Amateur and two Senior Opens, and both Lancaster[45] and Lehigh[46] help extend William Flynn's regional dominance.

NEW ENGLAND VARIATIONS

Connecticut golf majors on Yale University[47] but the southern part of the state – whose clubs are also part of the Metropolitan Golf Association – offers several more fine courses. These include a seaside Raynor/Tillinghast hybrid at the CC of Fairfield[48], its near neighbour Brooklawn[49], Willie Park Jnr's Woodway[50], Devereux Emmet's Wee Burn[51] and Charles Banks's virtually unaltered design at Tamarack[52].

The Redan in America
The National's 4th hole – the Nation's 1st

Chief among Charles Blair Macdonald's replica holes at the National Golf Links of America is the 4th – the Redan – which is modelled after the hole of the same name at Scotland's North Berwick Golf Club. The word 'redan' is a military one, drawn from a fortified position at Sebastopol, during the Crimean War. In golfing terms, it has generally translated to a reasonably long par three played to a green sloping prominently from right to left, and falling away notably at the back. The signature front-left bunker is invariably a steep and deep one – so much so that the North Berwick original was buttressed with wooden sleepers a good century before Pete Dye brought such things into vogue in America.

Macdonald's rendition at the National was America's first Redan, and was frequently imitated, initially by Macdonald himself (and his protégés Seth Raynor and Charles Banks) but later by all manner of architects in all sorts of locales, ranging from A.W. Tillinghast's 2nd at Somerset Hills (New Jersey) to Chandler Egan's rebuild of the 12th at Pebble Beach (see page 152). With classically minded modern designers still utilizing the template to this day, the Redan ranks, without question, as the single most-copied hole in the history of golf.

YALE GOLF COURSE

In the often overlooked world of collegiate golf facilities none has ever approached the challenge, scale and style of the golf course at Yale. When, in 1924, the widow of former Yale football star Ray Tompkins donated more than 700 acres of wooded land located just 1 mile west of the Yale Bowl, plans were quickly made to build a fitting golf course.

The cost of working on this hilly, rock-filled site was huge, with the eventual US$450,000 tab ranking Yale among the most expensive layouts yet built. To handle so large a project, the school turned to an older man whose place in the game's hierarchy was unassailable, Charles Blair Macdonald – though as with most of Macdonald's later architectural projects the actual creative work ended up being done primarily by his partner Seth Raynor. The result was a masterpiece of brawny, almost over-the-top design, with impressively wide fairways, enormous, wildly contoured greens and bunkers, which were not built with the undergraduate novice golfer in mind. Although there have been some regrettable alterations to the detail design of a few holes, Yale remains one of the most individual courses produced in an era of vision and invention.

NORTHERN NEW ENGLAND

The Boston area ranked closely with New York and Philadelphia for early golfing prominence and offers an impressive number of classic courses, topped by The Country Club but strongly bolstered by the timeless Myopia Hunt Club[53] (a four-time US Open venue in the early days), the short-but-fascinating Brae Burn[54] (another early US Open and Amateur site) and a quartet of important Donald Ross designs: Salem[55], Charles River[56], Winchester[57] and Essex County[58]. Early Boston resort-seekers often headed south to the coastline of Buzzard's Bay, where the William Flynn/Frederic Hood-designed Kittanset Club[59] occupies the tip of a windblown peninsula. While the links-like Sankaty Head[60] has been a long-time

The 1st hole at Baltimore Country Club's Five Farms Course is played over gently rolling ground to a rectangular period-piece green attended by two bunkers.

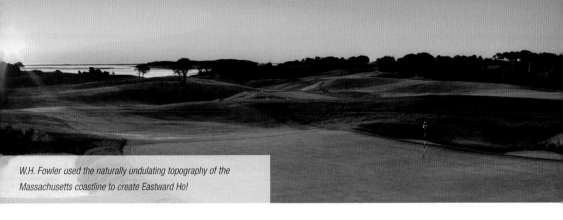

W.H. Fowler used the naturally undulating topography of the
Massachusetts coastline to create Eastward Ho!

favourite on Nantucket Island. On perennially
popular Cape Cod, a pair of classics, Ross's Oyster
Harbors[61] and Eastward Ho![62] are among the best.

EASTWARD HO!

Few American courses are as consistently testing
of a golfer's ability to play both the wind and the
often significant rolls of the terrain as Eastward
Ho! It is, very simply, one of the US's most natural
and attractive layouts, and a true testimonial to
the creative skills of the Englishman, W.H. Fowler.
He did not take up golf until he was 35, but he
became both a scratch player and an elite architect.
His design philosophy was once memorably
summed up as: 'God builds golf links, and the less
man meddles the better for all concerned.'

In the hands of a skilled practitioner, a less-is-
more approach to reshaping the native terrain is
inherently useful at two levels: it takes maximum
advantage of topographical subtleties while also
being cost-effective. As one of contemporary
design's great classicists, Tom Doak, has observed:
'The most noteworthy courses of the past decade
have been among the least expensive to build.'

Originally called the Chatham Country Club,
Eastward Ho! sits near Cape Cod's south-eastern
corner on a narrow, elevated spit of land. At only
6,356 yards, it is one of the most minimalist
courses ever created, its holes flowing with

seeming effortlessness over a wildly tumbling,
windblown landscape. Simply finding a solidly
playable routing was challenging enough here; that
Fowler created so many spectacular holes upon
which the skilled player can utilize the terrain
to gain an appreciable advantage is evidence of a
certain kind of genius. And the course has been
altered comparatively little since Fowler's day.

ELSEWHERE IN NEW ENGLAND

Central and western Massachusetts offer fewer
golf courses of excellence, though Ross designs
at Longmeadow[63] and Whitinsville[64] (widely
considered America's best nine-hole course), and
Mount Holyoke College's The Orchards[65] (site of
the 2004 US Women's Open) certainly stand out.

Neighbouring Rhode Island is tiny, but blessed
with a disproportionately large number of fine
early designs, largely because Donald Ross spent
his summers there during the 1920s. His layout at
Wannamoisett[66] – a veritable clinic on building a
world-class course on a tiny piece of land – has
long been viewed as the state's best, with his works
at Sakonnet[67] and the delightfully quirky Rhode
Island CC[68] following close behind. Ross even
had a hand in the historic Newport CC[69], though
the present layout (which hosted the 1995 US
Amateur and 2006 US Women's Open) owes far
more to a 1925 A.W. Tillinghast redesign.

While Vermont's Dorset Field Club[70] can claim to be America's oldest continuously active golf club (est. 1886), early Green Mountain golf featured largely player-friendly resort courses, with the Walter Travis/John Dunn-designed Ekwanok CC[71] remaining the state's finest course for more than a century. Neighbouring New Hampshire followed a similar path, its White Mountain region rating as America's leading summer destination at the turn of the 20th century, with the majority of courses being of the shorter, highly scenic variety. Maine differed little from this model, though several courses in its famed coastal region remain engaging period pieces, notably Bar Harbor's Kebo Valley[72] and Kennebunkport's Cape Arundel[73].

Upper New York State cannot be overlooked, particularly the Rochester area. Donald Ross dominated this region, where his much-altered East Course at Oak Hill[74] has hosted six Major championships, and the club's West Course as well as the nearby CC of Rochester[75] and Monroe CC[76] are all worthy Ross tests. Farther west, his underrated CC of Buffalo[77] and its neighbour, Charles Alison's Park CC[78], also set a particularly high prewar standard.

POSTWAR COURSES

The surge in suburban development after the war meant that suitable land was at a premium, but the occasional golf course of note was still built around major north-eastern cities. Throughout the region, designers such as Robert Trent Jones Snr, Dick Wilson, Hal Purdy and William Gordon attracted the lion's share of the work, generally completing bland (though often difficult) projects typical of the day. Rare period exceptions included Wilson's mid-1950s Long Island designs at Deepdale[79] and Meadowbrook[80], Gordon's Stanwich[81] and Jones's Black Hall[82] (both in Connecticut), Jones's rebuild of four-time Major

championship venue Congressional[83] (Maryland), and Wilson's Laurel Valley[84] (Pennsylvania), site of the 1965 PGA and 1989 US Senior Open.

RECENT DEVELOPMENTS

Modern development has generally been led by large-budget private clubs built in the outermost reaches of suburbia, distant enough to secure sufficient land but close enough to remain economically viable. In New York's heavily developed Westchester County, where sites are at a premium, Tom Fazio's Hudson National[85] and brother Jim's conversion of the former Briar Hall into Trump National[86] are generally rated the best of a limited crop. The story is considerably more impressive on Long Island. The Hamptons have further benefited from a pair of profusely bunkered Rees Jones layouts (Atlantic[87] and The Bridge[88]), as well as Bill Coore and Ben Crenshaw's more natural East Hampton GC[89]. But the limelight has been taken by a pair of new millennium additions, Tom Doak and Jack Nicklaus's Sebonack[90], and Bill Coore and Ben Crenshaw's spectacular north-shore creation, Friar's Head[91], both quickly establishing themselves among the nation's best.

FRIAR'S HEAD

Friar's Head successfully recaptures what the great American golf writer Max Behr once praised as golf-course architecture that is 'uncontaminated by the hand of man'. No greater compliment could be given to its architects, Bill Coore and Ben Crenshaw, who were selected by Ken Bakst in 1997 to build a course that embraced the design principles from the Golden Age of golf-course architecture.

Working with dunes that gave way to 200-foot bluffs overlooking Long Island Sound to the north and farmland with some natural depressions to the south, each nine in Coore and Crenshaw's routing starts and finishes in the dunes by the clubhouse.

Crucial to the overall success of the design is the way in which the dune and farmland areas were seamlessly knitted together.

Thanks to a wide-ranging variety of shapes, sizes and interior contours, the green complexes at Friar's Head are an equal match with those of the most-heralded Long Island courses.

OTHER MODERN COURSES

Northern New Jersey offers a solid collection of modern courses which includes: Tom Fazio's Ridge at Back Brook[92]; Michael Hurdzan and Dana Fry's impressively bunkered Hamilton Farm[93]; the recent addition to the Trump National family in Bedminster; and the Bayonne GC[94], a stunningly contrived links remarkably situated on the edge of New York harbour. The economic rebirth of Atlantic City has generated an even larger rush of modern development in the state's southern half, initially led by Robert Trent Jones's

Metedeconk National[95], then, more recently by Tom Fazio's Galloway National[96] and his Pine Valley homage, Pine Hill[97], and Bill Coore and Ben Crenshaw's tasteful Hidden Creek[98]. Pennsylvania has seen fewer modern layouts of note, though the Old Course at Stonewall[99], an early Tom Doak effort, can more than hold its own.

Maryland features a pair of high-profile contemporary courses: Caves Valley[100] in Owings Mills and Pete Dye's Bulle Rock[101], located in Havre de Grace. Outside Boston, Bill Coore and Ben Crenshaw's Olde Sandwich[102] and Gil Hanse's GC of Boston[103] rank as Massachusetts' finest postwar courses, while the more sparsely populated northern New England states still tend to rely mostly on resort development, with Maine's Sugarloaf GC[104] and a pair of Clive Clark designs – Maine's Belgrade Lakes GC[105] and New Hampshire's Lake Winnipesaukee CC[106] – ranking among the best of the new breed.

A meeting of minds for two of golf's great thinkers, Jack Nicklaus and Tom Doak, Sebonack exploits the natural movement of the land on this prime Long Island site.

The National
Southampton, New York

Has ever a golf course been saddled with a more presumptuous name? For those familiar with the life of its founder, Charles Blair Macdonald, no lesser title would have been fitting.

National Golf Links of America
Southampton, New York

Designer: Charles Blair Macdonald, 1911
Major events: Walker Cup 1922, 2013

Macdonald was one of the game's great figures and what he accomplished at the National changed the face of Stateside course design. Macdonald, ironically, was not even American, being born in Niagara Falls, Ontario in 1855 to a Scottish father and Canadian mother. He did, however, spend most of his life south of the border, growing up in Chicago before being sent to Scotland to study at St Andrews University in 1872.

THE ST ANDREWS INFLUENCE
Being introduced by his grandfather to a then not-so-Old Tom Morris, Macdonald fell in love with the game, quickly gaining sufficient proficiency to play regularly with Old Tom and his son, Young Tom Morris, the Strath brothers and other 19th-century Scottish golf dignitaries. With the seed deeply planted, Macdonald returned to America to spread the gospel of the Royal & Ancient game in his adopted homeland.

'It is a nod to the past, it is a nod to yesterday. I love that clubhouse. It is an ancient, brooding place. The land is brilliant and beautiful. You really feel like you are playing at a cousin to the golf courses of the British Isles. It has such great feeling and character.'
BEN CRENSHAW

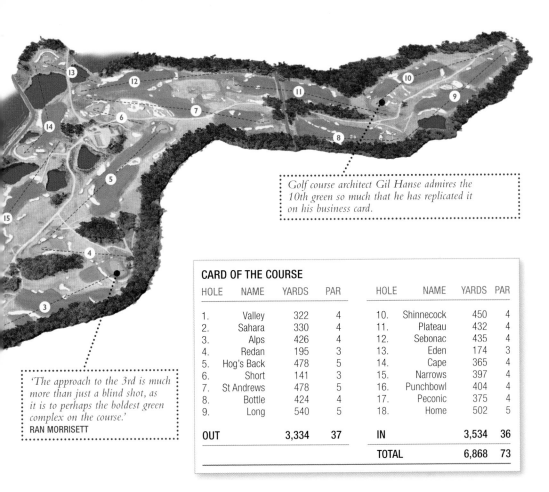

Golf course architect Gil Hanse admires the 10th green so much that he has replicated it on his business card.

'The approach to the 3rd is much more than just a blind shot, as it is to perhaps the boldest green complex on the course.'
RAN MORRISETT

CARD OF THE COURSE

HOLE	NAME	YARDS	PAR	HOLE	NAME	YARDS	PAR
1.	Valley	322	4	10.	Shinnecock	450	4
2.	Sahara	330	4	11.	Plateau	432	4
3.	Alps	426	4	12.	Sebonac	435	4
4.	Redan	195	3	13.	Eden	174	3
5.	Hog's Back	478	5	14.	Cape	365	4
6.	Short	141	3	15.	Narrows	397	4
7.	St Andrews	478	5	16.	Punchbowl	404	4
8.	Bottle	424	4	17.	Peconic	375	4
9.	Long	540	5	18.	Home	502	5
OUT		**3,334**	**37**	**IN**		**3,534**	**36**
				TOTAL		**6,868**	**73**

Macdonald's 1892 creation of the Chicago Golf Club did much to kick-start American golf, and his subsequent achievements (and pomposities) as the first official US Amateur champion, USGA guiding light, administrator and general father figure to the game's American development are well chronicled. But it was only after the turn of the 20th century that Macdonald set out to build the ideal golf course, a facility that would, in his words, 'serve as an incentive to the elevation of the game in America'.

STUDYING THE CLASSICS

For several years Macdonald laid his plans, revisiting Britain to study the most famous holes, hunting for the perfect site and putting together a list of affluent founder members that included no fewer than five US Amateur champions. After a search that ranged from Cape Cod to the very tip of Long Island, a rough, undulating property was procured in spring 1907. To aid in the building process, Macdonald hired a local Princeton-educated surveyor, Seth Raynor. Fortuitously,

Raynor, a non-golfer, quickly proved himself highly skilled in bringing blueprints to life. Raynor went on to become Macdonald's full-time partner and one of the Golden Age's most successful architects, ultimately completing more than 50 solo designs from New York to Hawaii, many of which remain golfing landmarks today.

DEFINING A PHILOSOPHY

At the National, Raynor executed a Macdonald plan that included replicating several of the finest holes in Great Britain, The intent was not to copy these holes precisely but to adapt their general tenets to the available land – an approach that both designers successfully carried on for the duration of their careers. Other holes were, in Macdonald's words, 'more or less composite', blending various appealing shots from the Old Country, while others were entirely original. Also of interest was the green contouring, for where no basic template was inherent to a particular hole's design, Macdonald often followed the advice of the great British player/writer Horace Hutchinson

Macdonald bought a windmill in Europe, had it re-erected and sent the bill to the member who suggested this addition to the course.

who, believing that man could never outdo nature, advocated dropping a handful of pebbles on a map of the proposed green, then sculpting its undulations to match their random pattern.

REPLICAS OF DISTINCTION

The first replica, the 2nd, is largely modelled after the late-lamented Sahara hole at Royal St George's, which was a blind par three played over what the eminent golf writer Bernard Darwin once called a 'heaving waste of sand'. Macdonald's de luxe version of Prestwick's celebrated Alps 17th is the 426-yard 3rd. Here, after a drive across a large diagonal bunker to a fairway that grows progressively narrower, the golfer is faced with a long, steeply uphill approach to a blind target. Of similarly thrilling appeal is the 4th, whose deep front-left bunker and sloping green mirror the famed Redan 15th at North Berwick.

At the 6th comes a classic Macdonald original, a slightly downhill 141-yarder requiring little muscle. Its challenge lies in a bunker-ringed putting surface marked by a pronounced horseshoe-shaped ridge – the Short's quirky trademark subsequently much imitated.

THE TURN

The 7th is Macdonald's adaptation of St Andrews' legendary Road hole, the principal differences being a sea of right-side sand replacing the original's notorious railway sheds, and a 5-foot deep bunker flanking the rear of the putting surface in place of the much-feared road. But it is the hole's central ingredient – the greenside Road bunker itself – that lingers longest in the memory, for it is configured more like a mineshaft than a sand hazard. Though somewhat shallower today than in days of yore, it surely remains among the most dangerous golfing hazards in all of North America. Now approaching the southern reaches

The approach to the 397-yard 15th, with the National's famed windmill in the distance and a small pond hidden behind the elevated putting surface.

of the property, the golfer encounters the split-fairway 8th, where a narrower left-side option affords the best angle of approach, and the 540-yard 9th, a gently uphill hole modelled loosely after the 14th at St Andrews.

Of particular architectural significance is the 11th, for it was here that Macdonald introduced another staple of his repertoire, the double-plateau green. Here the front-left and back-right segments are elevated, creating numerous interesting pin placements as well as something of a 'slot' for over-struck approaches to run through the putting surface into a single rear bunker.

The 13th replicates the 11th at St Andrews, the influential par three colloquially referred to as the Eden. The primary components of the hole – a steeply sloping green fronted by two dangerous bunkers – were easy enough for Macdonald to recreate, but what of the backing estuary? Lacking a comparable water hazard, he instead built a long, narrow bunker beyond the putting surface.

THE ORIGINAL CAPE

Though much altered from its initial design, the 14th at the National is one of Macdonald's most famous original creations. His initial version measured just over 300 yards and curved along an inlet of Bullhead Bay, its 'Cape' green jutting excitingly out into the water. Wary of equipment advances rendering it drivable, Macdonald moved the putting surface to its present site in the mid-1920s.

After climbing to high ground, the world-renowned 17th beckons. This relatively short two-shotter runs downhill, with the waters of Peconic Bay providing a wide panoramic backdrop. Like any great strategic hole it offers multiple options off the tee, though the fundamental test is to open up the best angle of approach by hugging the left side of the fairway. The National concludes with an uphill par five, which Bernard Darwin once rated the finest finisher in the world.

Fishers Island
Fishers Island, New York

Although not an international household name in golf circles, the Fishers Island Club occupies a lofty perch among golf-design aficionados, its delightfully secluded waterfront layout representing one of the finest and least-altered courses of American golf architecture's vaunted Golden Age.

Fishers Island Club
Fishers Island, New York

Designer: Seth Raynor, 1926

Fishers Island has been called the 'Cypress Point of the East', but its members know it as 'The Big Club' as there is also a 9-hole course on the island.

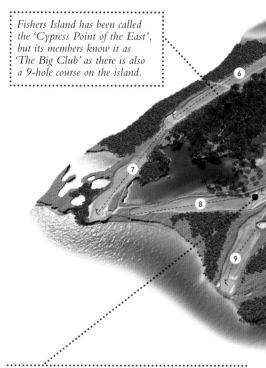

Great acclaim for this course has hardly been a constant; indeed, Fishers Island long maintained such quiet anonymity that the most established of American golf publications – a magazine with its headquarters little more than an hour from the club – managed to overlook the course entirely in each of its biannual Top 100 rankings from 1975 to 2000. Thankfully, the Fishers Island membership was atypical in their reaction to the slight, being happy enough with their own splendid links to ignore such trendy options as calling in Robert Trent Jones to 'modernize' things or throwing a lavish party for ratings panellists. Instead the club quietly carried on, unconcerned with what the so-called 'experts' thought, and in the end, inevitably, its greatness was well and fully recognized.

NEW YORK OR CONNECTICUT?

Fishers Island enjoys one of golf's more idyllic locales, occupying the eastern end of an island that,

The 8th hole favours a fade on the tee shot and a draw on the approach, a formula repeated many times by Pete Dye during his career.

though situated nearly within shouting distance of the Connecticut shoreline, manages through some ancient geographic quirk, to be a part of New York State. A resort hotbed during the late 19th century, it was redeveloped as a private summer retreat during the mid-1920s, modelled after what would become its long-time seasonal sister club, Mountain Lake in Lake Wales, Florida. Smartly, Fishers Island followed its sibling's successful lead in two important ways: hiring the famed landscape design firm of Frederick Law Olmsted

to masterplan the island; and retaining golf-course architect Seth Raynor to design its spectacular oceanfront links.

By the time the Fishers Island Club approached Raynor, he had established rather an envied status within the architecture world because of his partnership with the renowned course designer Charles Blair Macdonald, landing all manner of high-society projects in Florida, New York and, eventually, the Midwest and Hawaii. Sticking with the established Macdonald

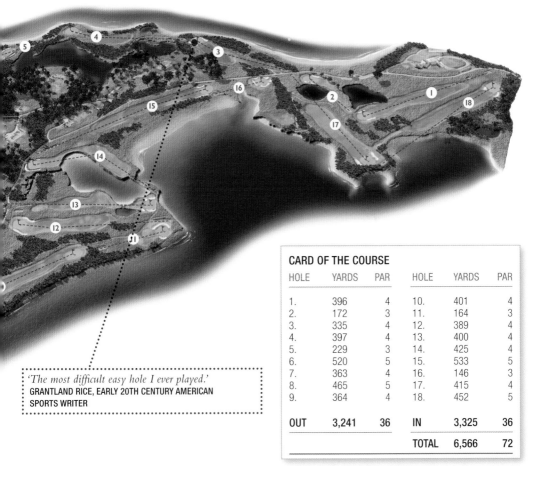

> 'The most difficult easy hole I ever played.'
> GRANTLAND RICE, EARLY 20TH CENTURY AMERICAN SPORTS WRITER

CARD OF THE COURSE

HOLE	YARDS	PAR	HOLE	YARDS	PAR
1.	396	4	10.	401	4
2.	172	3	11.	164	3
3.	335	4	12.	389	4
4.	397	4	13.	400	4
5.	229	3	14.	425	4
6.	520	5	15.	533	5
7.	363	4	16.	146	3
8.	465	5	17.	415	4
9.	364	4	18.	452	5
OUT	3,241	36	IN	3,325	36
			TOTAL	6,566	72

The 229-yard Biarritz 5th, requiring a well-struck long-iron or fairway metal to carry the chasm and reach the bunkered green.

formula, Raynor replicated great holes from the Old World, a technique that, combined with the quasi-geometric stylings of his squarish greens and angular bunkers, gives his courses a splendidly old-fashioned appeal today. At Fishers Island, this classic ambience is enhanced by the paucity of housing along the course's perimeter and by the general distinctiveness of the property, for its tumbling, links-like terrain offers ocean views from every hole and all the coastline any designer might wish to employ.

A FAST GETAWAY

Several of the club's most recognized holes come during an early march along the island's southern shoreline, beginning with the 172-yard 2nd (the rare Redan replica to be played across a pond) and the 335-yard 3rd, a potentially drivable par four that curves gently right and climbs to a skyline green sited above the beach. A laid-up tee shot will leave only a short pitch here, but with 10-foot deep, grass-faced bunkers flanking the green on three

sides danger lies eminently close at hand. The 397-yard 4th then continues along the coastline and is a palpably exciting affair, with most drives to its plateau fairway facing an approach of the Alps variety – that is, an uphill shot to a green almost completely hidden behind a large, rough-covered hill. A fine strategic element lies in the fact that a glimpse of the green can be had from the fairway's far right side, but the drive must flirt with a brush-filled plunge to the beach in order to gain such an advantage.

THE BIARRITZ

Fishers Island's definitive hole must surely be the 229-yard 5th, a wonderful rendition of perhaps the Macdonald/Raynor standard, the Biarritz. These demanding par threes were patterned after a long-deceased cliff-top hole in Biarritz, France, and feature a large putting surface fronted by a deep swale, with narrow, symmetrical bunkers along either side. The French original required an initial carry over a deep coastal chasm, something the seaside Fishers Island version uniquely matches among the hole's many 20th-century inland replicas.

Another pre-eminent front-nine hole is the 465-yard 8th, a short, into-the-wind par five roughly modelled after the Road hole at St Andrews. Here a stretch of scrub-lined beach substitutes for the original's railway sheds in protecting the optimum right side of the fairway, the area from which the green's deep Road bunker can best be avoided. The 401-yard 10th also challenges the prevailing breeze, and features a crowned, bunkerless putting surface built to repel any ball not played assertively into its heart.

THE BACK NINE

The finest hole on the back nine may well be the 164-yard 11th, a thrillingly windblown adaptation of the 11th at St Andrews, complete with deep bunkers to mimic the original Hill and Strath, and complemented by the expanse of East Harbor as an Eden estuary-like backdrop. Also noteworthy are the 400-yard 13th and 425-yard 14th, the former played to another seaside green defended by sand and water, the latter a tough dogleg left around a coastal lagoon that, given today's enhanced equipment, just might be drivable under favourable conditions.

A singular criticism of Fishers Island – that too many greens sport perfectly symmetrical, left-and-right greenside bunkering – might be applied to the 533-yard 15th and the 415-yard 17th, though both are amply challenging and situated attractively alongside the harbour. The 146-yard 16th also merits a mention, being a downhill, over-water rendition of Charles Blair Macdonald's original Short hole, the 6th at the National Golf Links of America. It might be observed that the 452-yard 18th, while featuring a superbly contoured green, is not the grandest of finishers. However, this cannot be blamed on Seth Raynor, who originally built both the 18th and the beachside 8th as difficult par fours (at 433 and 418 yards respectively), but the membership later opted to lengthen them. In the bigger picture, such alterations are minor and seem trivial at Fishers Island, where panoramic beauty and classic replica-oriented design continue to rank Raynor's golf course high among America's very best.

No fewer than twelve holes at Fishers Island are routed beside the rocky shoreline. This is the 7th green.

Winged Foot
Mamaroneck, New York

Named after the popular logo of the New York Athletic Club, from where its founding members came, Winged Foot was intended for big things right from its inception, beginning with the selection of a top designer for its golf courses – Albert Warren ('A.W.') Tillinghast.

**Winged Foot Golf Club
(West course)**
Mamaroneck, New York

Designer: A.W. Tillinghast, 1923
Major events: US Open 1929, 1959, 1974, 1984, 2006; USPGA 1997;
US Amateur 1940, 2004; Walker Cup 1949

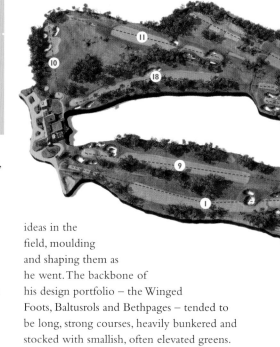

A dominant figure in regional architectural circles, Tillinghast was one of the Golden Age's great all-rounders, having played the game quite well, written about it extensively, edited perhaps its finest-ever American magazine (*Golf Illustrated*) and been a highly successful agronomist, all in addition to building first-class courses from coast to coast. Tilly, as he was commonly known, was also one of golf's epic characters. Coming from an affluent Philadelphia family, he avoided education almost entirely, yet still possessed the resources necessary to travel extensively, get driven daily to his Manhattan office by chauffeured limousine and, through it all, drink copiously.

Eschewing the drawing of detailed plans, Tillinghast was a man who developed his design ideas in the field, moulding and shaping them as he went. The backbone of his design portfolio – the Winged Foots, Baltusrols and Bethpages – tended to be long, strong courses, heavily bunkered and stocked with smallish, often elevated greens. Beyond that, Tillinghast's course designs also possess a hard-to-define aesthetic component - 'Tillinghast polish' – which has long given them an aura of stylish grandeur.

CARD OF THE COURSE

HOLE	NAME	YARDS	PAR	HOLE	NAME	YARDS	PAR
1.	Genesis	450	4	10.	Pulpit	188	3
2.	Elm	453	4	11.	Billows	396	4
3.	Pinnacle	216	3	12.	Cape	640	5
4.	Sound View	469	4	13.	White Mule	214	3
5.	Long Lane	515	5	14.	Shamrock	458	4
6.	El	321	4	15.	Pyramid	416	4
7.	Babe-in-the-Woods	162	3	16.	Hells-Bells	478	4
8.	Arena	475	4	17.	Well-Well	449	4
9.	Meadow	514	4	18.	Revelations	450	4
OUT		**3,575**	**35**	**IN**		**3,689**	**35**
				TOTAL		**7,264**	**70**

'Every hole, barring the one-shotters, seems quite innocent and without guile from the teeing ground, and it is only the knowledge that the next shot must be played with rifle accuracy that brings the realization that the drive must be placed.'
A.W. TILLINGHAST

During the 1959 US Open Billy Casper single putted nine consecutive greens, starting at the 15th in the 3rd round. The last of them, on the 5th in the final round, was the longest. He went on to win.

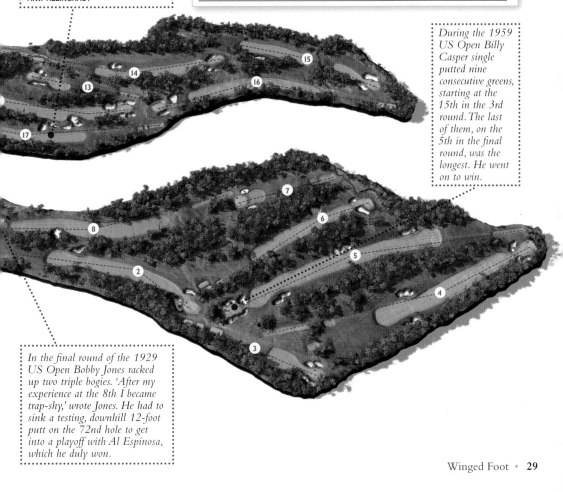

In the final round of the 1929 US Open Bobby Jones racked up two triple bogies. 'After my experience at the 8th I became trap-shy,' wrote Jones. He had to sink a testing, downhill 12-foot putt on the 72nd hole to get into a playoff with Al Espinosa, which he duly won.

DESIGN PHILOSOPHY

At Winged Foot, Tilly found 280 rolling, partially wooded acres dotted with large formations of ledge rock, some of which were dynamited, the remainder serving as foundations for many of the club's more elevated putting surfaces. Famously instructed by the founders to 'Give us a man-sized course', Tillinghast responded with 36 epic holes, virtually all of which amply demonstrated his belief that 'a controlled shot to a closely guarded green is the surest test of a man's golf'. At Winged Foot, however, he outdid himself by building some of the most heavily contoured putting surfaces in his design portfolio and configuring them in ways designed to favour approach shots played from specific fairway angles, thus creating somewhat more driving strategy than might be apparent at first glance.

Within the club membership, opinion has long been closely divided as to which course is better. The West is unquestionably longer and tougher, as complete an examination of a great golfer's skills as exists in the United States. But the East Course nips closely at its heels, lacking a bit of distance, certainly, but possessing far more variety and general playing interest.

A FEARSOME START

The 1st is one of the toughest opening holes in golf. Bending slightly leftward the fairway is no simple target and the green is a terror, sloped steeply from back to front, dangerously contoured within, and flanked by long, deep bunkers on both sides. The it is the left side of the 2nd fairway which offers the optimum line of approach to a larger green angled left-to-right behind another notably deep bunker. It is followed by one of America's toughest par threes, the 216-yard 3rd, which plays slightly uphill to a startlingly narrow, bunker-flanked green.

A BRIEF RESPITE

The downhill 469-yard 4th, once a marathon in days of old, is today fairly reasonable, paving the way for three shorter holes that, as a group, represent the golfer's lone sustained opportunity to pick up strokes. The front nine closes with the 9th, a manageable par five for members which gained an element of notoriety in 2006 when a USGA trying desperately to keep up with unchecked equipment advances stretched it to a par four of 514 yards – the longest two-shotter in Major championship history.

TILLY'S BEST

Tillinghast was a designer known for the richness of his par threes and Winged Foot's 10th is universally rated among his very best. Once described by the great golfer Ben Hogan as a 'three-iron into some guy's bedroom' (in reference to a home that *looks* especially close to the green), it is today more of a five or six played to a steeply sloping putting surface built in the shape of an upside-down pear. On both sides of the green the terrain falls immediately away, left and right towards nasty bunkers. The back of the green, though substantially wider, is also no bargain. Tilly himself reportedly called this the best par three he ever built. A golfer would, at any rate, be hard pressed to find many that surpass it.

THE FINAL PAR FIVE

There follows a modest respite, for the better player needs only an iron and wedge at the 11th, and the 12th – despite being extended to 640 yards for the 2006 US Open – is the tournament layout's final par five. The difficult 13th, playing slightly uphill to another notably narrow green, represents the last of the par threes, and then begins a closing run of five two-shotters that, particularly in Major championship

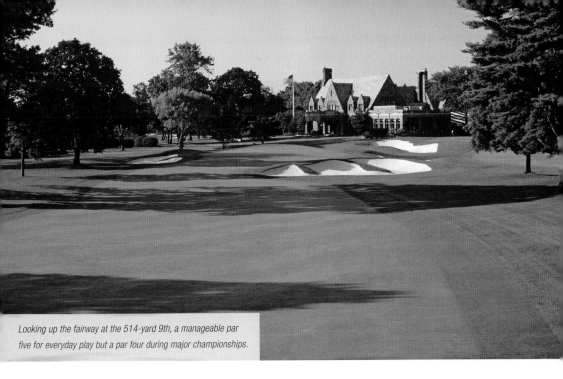

Looking up the fairway at the 514-yard 9th, a manageable par five for everyday play but a par four during major championships.

conditions, truly separate the serious contenders from those merely cashing cheques.

Ranking among the more striking holes at Winged Foot is the dogleg-left 14th, its drive flirting with a single left-side trap, its second travelling uphill to a left-to-right sloping green guarded by sand and several overhanging trees. At 416 yards, the 15th is the shortest of the finishers but plays deceptively long.

TURNING FOR HOME

The 478-yard 16th is another par five converted to two-shot status for Major championship play and, much like the 9th, the switch abruptly transforms it from pleasant to vicious. A personal favourite of Jack Nicklaus's, the 449-yard 17th may seem short by comparison, but plays only slightly easier, its tee shot requiring a fade past a cluster of bunkers to a left-to-right curving fairway.

MEMORABLE FINISH

As arduous as holes 14–17 may be they largely pale in comparison to the challenge and individuality of the 450-yard 18th, one of America's most historic finishers. A sweeping dogleg left, this demanding, tree-lined test requires the tee shot to evade a modern-era bunker. The approach is then played to an elevated, false-fronted green that, notably, is the only one on the West Course where sand is not a primary hazard. The putting surface is steeply pitched with a prominent rise in its front-right section defending a tricky Sunday pin position. The biggest danger to the approach is a false front, for balls coming up even slightly short will roll back into the fairway and shots lost right (an uphill chip from deep rough), long (a scary downhill chip or putt) or left (the green's lone relevant sand) often present even greater dilemmas, making the 18th a truly unforgiving hole.

Bethpage Black
Farmingdale, New York

In 1935, near the height of America's Great Depression, legendary architect A. W. Tillinghast received a very prestigious government project: a Works Progress Administration (WPA) undertaking on Long Island that would eventually become the grandest municipal golf facility ever built in the United States. It was for Bethpage State Park.

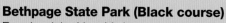

Bethpage State Park (Black course)
Farmingdale, New York

Designer: A.W. Tillinghast, 1936
Major events: US Open 2002, 2009

'Without doubt, were the other three courses at Bethpage as severe as Black, the place would not enjoy the great popularity it has known. If they had to play under such punishing conditions week in and out, they'd probably chuck their clubs into the lake and take to pitching horeshoes.'
A.W. TILLINGHAST

The brainchild of a headstrong and controversial New York State parks commissioner named Robert Moses, the Bethpage project involved the acquisition (and subsequent renovation by Tillinghast) of the Devereux Emmet-designed private Lenox Hills Country Club, the construction of three additional Tillinghast courses on the site and, some two decades later, the addition of a fifth and final course that was laid out by A.H. Tull. Of the four Tillinghast designs, three started in 1935, but it was the launch in 1936 of the fourth, the

highly ambitious Black Course, that attracted so much attention to the new megafacility on Long Island.

A GENUINE TILLINGHAST?
It must be noted that Tillinghast's status as the primary designer of the Black Course has occasionally been questioned, with some suggesting that credit should actually go to the property's manager, Joseph Burbeck. The preponderance of evidence, however, fails to

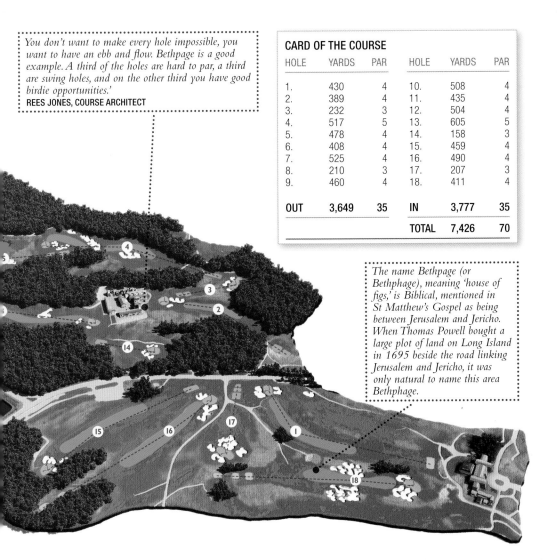

CARD OF THE COURSE

HOLE	YARDS	PAR	HOLE	YARDS	PAR
1.	430	4	10.	508	4
2.	389	4	11.	435	4
3.	232	3	12.	504	4
4.	517	5	13.	605	5
5.	478	4	14.	158	3
6.	408	4	15.	459	4
7.	525	4	16.	490	4
8.	210	3	17.	207	3
9.	460	4	18.	411	4
OUT	**3,649**	**35**	**IN**	**3,777**	**35**
			TOTAL	**7,426**	**70**

The name Bethpage (or Bethphage), meaning 'house of figs,' is Biblical, mentioned in St Matthew's Gospel as being between Jerusalem and Jericho. When Thomas Powell bought a large plot of land on Long Island in 1695 beside the road linking Jerusalem and Jericho, it was only natural to name this area Bethphage.

support such assertions, though Tillinghast did credit Burbeck with initiating the concept of making the Black Course 'something which might compare with Pine Valley as a great test'. Remarkably, in many ways, the course at Bethpage State Park actually succeeded in doing just that.

The Black Course is built over sandy, rolling terrain at least somewhat akin to that of Pine Valley and, save for the opening two and closing three holes, is routed through similarly dense woods. Its bunkering and overall length were created on a comparable scale, leaving only its relatively benign greens significantly different. For some, this latter point is suggestive of Joseph Burbeck's alleged design role, though a far more likely scenario is that Burbeck's inexperienced WPA work crews constructed greens without the benefit of either detailed plans (which Tillinghast seldom employed) or the frequently travelling architect's direct supervision.

For many years the Black existed as something of a local legend, recognized throughout the New York metropolitan area as a layout whose difficulty could match anything in the north-east, yet whose municipal course upkeep rendered it something of an afterthought at the national level. But in an effort to put a more attractive face on municipal golf, the USGA broke with decades of private club tradition by awarding Bethpage the 2002 US Open. To renovate the facility in preparation for this event, it went into partnership with New York State and architect Rees Jones.

THE RE-EMERGENCE OF A CHAMPIONSHIP COURSE

Restored to a championship level of conditioning for the landmark event, the Black is today a bona fide powerhouse, a layout virtually devoid of weak holes and well stocked with many of a world-class nature. Perhaps the best of the bunch is the 517-yard 4th, a prodigious two-shotter that requires the aggressive player to drive across a large left-side bunker if the green is to be reached in two, but also allows those laying up to decide among multiple strategic options on their second.

The 478-yard 5th is another exacting hole, requiring a prodigious carry over sand to reach the optimum right side of the fairway, from which a long, uphill approach remains over two deep bunkers fronting the green. Then the dogleg-right, 525-yard 7th is similarly thought-provoking, daring a drive across another huge fairway bunker if the green is to be approached in two. For its

On the 4th tee the golfer is challenged to take on the left-hand bunker if the distant green is to be reached in two shots.

Rees Jones's re-bunkering of the 18th hole is controversial in terms of style, although effective for a major championship.

part, the 210-yard 8th bears a certain stylistic resemblance to the 14th at Pine Valley, but despite being sharply downhill and having a pond, it is actually a very different hole altogether.

THE BACK NINE

The inward half is most notable for a series of tremendously long par fours, beginning with the heavily bunkered 508-yard 10th, a real monster requiring a long approach over a valley to an elevated green. The 504-yard 12th turns sharply left around an ultra-invasive corner bunker, while the most engaging hole in the back nine may well be the 158-yard 14th, which plays over a wide depression to a green angled behind a deep front-right bunker. The 459-yard 15th, with its steeply elevated, two-tiered green, is commonly rated the Black's single toughest hole. The run of gruelling two-shotters ends with the 490-yard downhill

16th, setting up to a difficult penultimate test, the 207-yard 17th, whose shallow green is surrounded by five large bunkers.

The 411-yard 18th is a moderate finisher effectively illustrating both the pluses and minuses of Rees Jones's pre-Open modernization work. Jones was able to build nearly 40 more yards of length onto an otherwise short closing hole, which was a substantial improvement for Major championship play. On the downside, his 'restored' bunkering, both fairway and greenside, is manifestly overdone, little resembling Tillinghast's original hazards and giving the hole – and, sadly, a number of others – a sort of Florida-with-fescue feel.

Still, Bethpage remains an inspiringly grand design, conceived and built on a scale that few courses (virtually none of them public) can match, and it acquitted itself notably well during Tiger Woods' three-shot 2002 victory.

Shinnecock Hills
Southampton, New York

'This is finally going to be a great Open. They couldn't trick it up. It is out there in its natural state and there is nothing they can do about it.'
RAY FLOYD, 1986 US OPEN CHAMPION AT SHINNECOCK HILLS

Though several more loosely organized American golf clubs played the game sooner, Long Island's Shinnecock Hills can claim to be the nation's first incorporated golfing entity. That its incorporation is of relevance is entirely appropriate given that its founders were three prominent New York businessmen.

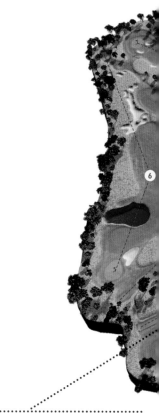

Shinnecock Hills Golf Club
Southampton, New York

Designers: William Flynn and Howard Toomey, 1931
Major events: US Open 1896, 1986, 1995, 2004;
US Amateur 1896; US Women's Amateur 1900;
Walker Cup 1977

CARD OF THE COURSE

HOLE	NAME	YARDS	PAR	HOLE	NAME	YARDS	PAR
1.	Westward Ho	393	4	10.	Eastward Ho	412	4
2.	Plateau	226	3	11.	Hill Head	158	3
3.	Peconic	478	4	12.	Tuckahoe	468	4
4.	Pump House	435	4	13.	Road Side	370	4
5.	Montauk	537	5	14.	Thom's Elbow	443	4
6.	Pond	474	4	15.	Sebonac	403	4
7.	Redan	189	3	16.	Shinnecock	540	5
8.	Lowlands	398	4	17.	Eden	179	3
9.	Ben Nevis	443	4	18.	Home	450	4
OUT		**3,573**	**35**	**IN**		**3,423**	**35**
				TOTAL		**6,996**	**70**

'Gentlemen, this beats rifle shooting for distance and accuracy. It's a game that I think would go in our country.'
WILLIAM VANDERBILT, FOUNDER MEMBER OF THE SHINNECOCK HILLS GOLF CLUB

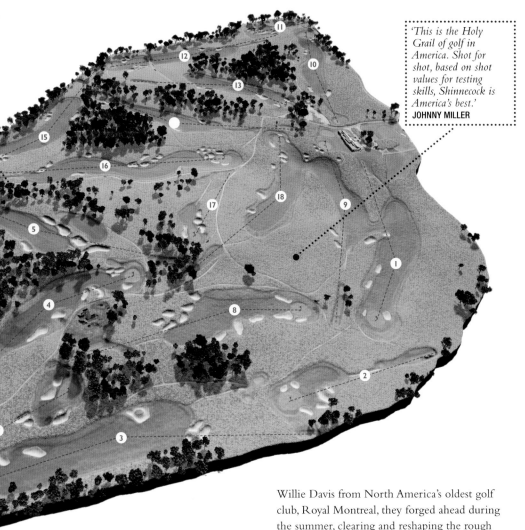

While on holiday in Biarritz during the winter of 1891, New Yorkers William Vanderbilt, Duncan Cryder and Edward Mead saw a demonstration of golf by the Scottish professional Willie Dunn. Enthralled, they returned to America determined to build what they likely believed to be the US's first course. Borrowing professional/architect Willie Davis from North America's oldest golf club, Royal Montreal, they forged ahead during the summer, clearing and reshaping the rough native landscape to make a 12-hole layout that was ready by late August. The official date of incorporation was 21 September 1891.

DESIGN EVOLUTION

A nine-hole women's course was added two years later, and the men's layout was expanded to 18 holes by Willie Dunn in 1895. Shinnecock hosted the second US Amateur and Open in 1896 but dropped out of the national tournament limelight immediately. With the arrival of the livelier rubber-core ball rendering the early course obsolete, Charles Blair Macdonald and Seth Raynor designed a new 6,108-yard layout in 1916, remnants of which still dot the club's practice areas today. Finally, when the 1930 expansion of state Route 27 forced yet another change, the club hired William Flynn to create the Shinnecock Hills layout that has now stood among the world's elite for 80 years.

THE FLYNN LAYOUT

William Flynn was provided with new land to the north on which to build his new course, though several pieces of its Macdonald/Raynor predecessor were retained. Flynn worked in partnership with his faithful engineer/business manager Howard Toomey, and a construction crew that included future architects William Gordon and Dick Wilson.

AN UNPREDICTABLE WIND

Several factors combine to give Shinnecock a playing ambience unlike any other American golf course. First is the wind, not only because it blows steadily but also because the term 'prevailing' is of limited relevance here. Though a south-west breeze is most likely, other conditions are common, their effect heightened by a routing that runs in every direction imaginable, with consecutive holes in the same direction on only three occasions.

Then there is the rough, a sea of knee-high, golden brown native grass which has delineated these links since the beginning. Finally there is the layout's spaciousness, for while many holes run parallel, there is generally so much room between them that the golfer scarcely notices.

A GENTLE GETAWAY

Playing out of America's first golf clubhouse – built in 1892 by celebrated New York society architect Stanford White – Shinnecock begins on high ground, with the relatively benign 1st running downhill. The challenge picks up immediately at the 2nd, a slightly uphill one-shotter with a line of three bunkers to be carried in front of the putting surface.

Little altered since its days as Macdonald/Raynor's 13th, the 3rd requires a strong tee shot to reach a level lie on the gently downhill fairway. The 4th then turns back, often playing harder than its predecessor because of a pair of insidious right-side fairway bunkers, an aggressively contoured green and a prevailing headwind. Known as the Pond hole, the 6th began life as a short three-shotter, with sand dunes flanking its right, an alternative left-side fairway and a prominent water hazard crossing 75 yards from the green. Today the dunes are gone and the left-side fairway represents little more than a safe area for shorter hitters, yet the remaining 215-yard sand carry to the right fairway is not easy.

THE REDAN

The 7th was Macdonald and Raynor's 14th hole. Flynn chose to retain their original Redan concept but reshaped the green complex, narrowing the front-right entrance with bunkers, which makes an all-carry approach safer than a run-up. With the right-to-left fall of the putting surface demonstrating typical Redan severity, this can be a dangerous test.

To close the outward half comes the difficult 443-yard 9th, a slight dogleg left requiring a drive to a rolling fairway, then a long second to an elevated green pitched into a broad slope below the clubhouse.

During the 2004 US Open the USGA had to water greens such as the 7th during play to keep them even vaguely playable.

AN ELITE NINE

Many rate Shinnecock's back nine the best in American golf and the 10th kicks it off impressively. Decision-making begins on the tee: does a golfer use a fairway metal and safely lay up on a crest some 240 yards out or try to blast a driver down the fairly steep plunge that follows? The former leaves a 160-yard approach over a valley to another starkly elevated green, the latter an uphill pitch – but to be caught in purgatory on the downhill slope in between means trouble.

Entirely different in character is the notable 11th. Played straight uphill to a small skyline green, it is guarded left by a long bunker and front-right by three of the deepest hazards on the course. Requiring little more than a short-iron, this green is a particularly wind-exposed target offering no easy options.

Playing from an elevated tee located only feet behind the clubhouse, the 14th begins with a downhill drive to a fairway pinched by sand at the 300-yard mark. The approach is uphill to a smallish green situated in a saddle, with rough- and tree-covered hillsides converging from both sides. Compounding the challenge is a putting surface falling away from the player, guarded short by four bunkers carved into the grade.

Running in entirely different directions the final threesome take full advantage of the wind. Usually facing a stiff headwind, the 16th is a full three-shotter with a left-side bunker cluster in play on the second shot. No fewer than ten bunkers guard this narrow putting surface.

THE FINISHERS

Turning to the north-west, the 17th plays to a green angled right-to-left behind a line of three bunkers. This design template appears frequently on Flynn courses but is particularly tricky at this juncture, for the prevailing wind is blowing left-to-right, demanding a hard draw into the breeze (and towards the bunkers) to access any left-side pin. Returning to the south-east, the breeze and general flow of the terrain favour a tee shot played up the right side of the 18th. From here the golfer is left with a mid-iron to a sloping but reasonably open green, bunkered right and left but not immediately short.

Maidstone
East Hampton, New York

For more than half a century, the Hamptons' three great golfing clubs – Shinnecock Hills, the National and Maidstone – were always spoken of together, viewed on a nearly equal status as the Holy Trinity of Long Island golf.

Maidstone Golf Club
East Hampton, New York

Designer: Willie Park Jnr, 1922

Though still ranked firmly among America's finest courses, Maidstone today lies somewhat in the shadows of Southampton golf, following the US Open's triumphant return to Shinnecock Hills in 1986 and America's newfound interest in classic course design re-elevating the National Golf Links to pre-eminent status as the place where the Golden Age of architecture all began.

Located some 12 miles east of its higher-profile neighbours, Maidstone occupies an enviable, if slightly disjointed, property along Long Island's southern shore, a site that includes

CARD OF THE COURSE					
HOLE	YARDS	PAR	HOLE	YARDS	PAR
1.	380	4	10.	382	4
2.	537	5	11.	422	4
3.	408	4	12.	179	3
4.	171	3	13.	490	5
5.	325	4	14.	148	3
6.	403	4	15.	493	5
7.	335	4	16.	471	5
8.	151	3	17.	328	4
9.	402	4	18.	378	4
OUT	3,112	35	IN	3,291	37
			TOTAL	6,403	72

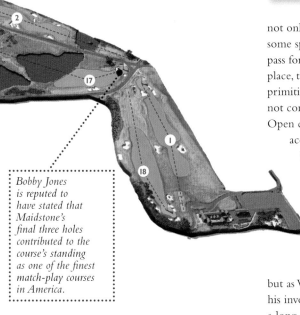

Bobby Jones is reputed to have stated that Maidstone's final three holes contributed to the course's standing as one of the finest match-play courses in America.

Despite Maidstone's privacy policy and its shunning of publicity, the club is still respected by the golfing press, even in the face of stiff competition, retaining 100th place in Golf Digest's 2013 ranking of the top courses in America.

not only a bit of flattish inland terrain but also some splendid oceanside land that, in spots, might pass for genuine links. A low-key, family-oriented place, the club began playing golf over three purely primitive holes in 1894. The present layout did not come into being until 1922, when two-time Open champion Willie Park Jnr utilized the newly acquired seaside tract to create a diminutive but exceedingly interesting 18-hole course.

WILLIE PARK JNR

Willie Park Jnr (along with his brother Jack) had previously been credited with helping Maidstone member Adrian Larkin build the club's initial 18-hole course back in 1899, but as Willie Park spent all of that year in Britain his involvement could not have been more than a long-distance consultation. By the early 1920s, however, Willie Park was residing full-time in the United States and doing much of his best design work – that same year of 1922, for example, also seeing the completion of perhaps his best-known American project, the North Course at Olympia Fields, in suburban Chicago. Alas, because of frequent design-related travel, Willie Park had never managed to see the finished Maidstone course when he suffered a nervous breakdown in summer 1923. He soon returned home to Scotland, where he died, essentially in a state of dementia, two years later.

PLAYING OUT TO THE DUNES

Following a forthright 380-yard opener, Park's Maidstone design hits its stride at the 537-yard 2nd, a straight hole flanked closely on its left by Dunemere Road (out-of-bounds) and played to an angled green modelled loosely on that of the well-known Road hole at St Andrews. The 408-yard 3rd is another solid test – routed dead into the prevailing wind, its green small and heavily bunkered – before the wide expanse of Hook pond is encountered and the challenge picks up in earnest.

With the pond being far too wide to drive across (particularly in 1922), the 171-yard 4th hole was created by building a mid-water tee on a narrow isthmus, which connects to the southern banks via a long bridge. This well-bunkered one-shotter is followed by the tricky 5th, a 325-yard drive-and-pitch played to a two-level green backed flush against the pond. Front-right

Maidstone's English-style clubhouse overlooks the ocean.

pins (tucked beyond a small bunker) are tricky, but back placements (perched on the top tier, with water just beyond) will test the nerves of any player. Continuing southwards into the breeze, the 403-yard 6th is a foretaster for a run of holes once referred to by the celebrated golf writer Bernard Darwin as 'the finest stretch I have seen in America'.

The fun begins with the 335-yard 7th, a dogleg right carved tightly along the edge of the pond that, despite the long carry into the prevailing headwind, is potentially drivable. Then the 151-yard 8th runs directly into the oceanside dunes, its small, tightly bunkered green somewhat hidden by a huge sand hill cutting in from the right. Recalling the great blind par threes of the UK, it is a throwback in the truest sense.

Impressive as the 8th may be, however, it is the 402-yard 9th that many consider Maidstone's best. Running nearly parallel to the beach, its fairway slithers between large dunes (the massive left-side hill was actually built by Willie Park) before climbing to an elevated, windswept green angled left to right around a 10-foot deep bunker. The 382-yard 10th then backtracks westwards through the sand hills, its similarly exposed hill-top green guarded short-left by five smaller bunkers and long by a steep slope.

RETURNING TO THE SEA

After briefly detouring inland at the 422-yard 11th and 179-yard 12th, play returns to the sea at the 490-yard 13th, an into-the-wind par five whose long, narrow green sits among the dunes, flanked left by a deep, grass-faced bunker. This is just a warm-up, however, for Maidstone's second world-renowned hole, the idyllic 148-yard 14th. For here stands a tricky little one-shotter that would be at home on even the finest British links, a tiny, windblown test that is 100 per cent carry

A view of the raised 9th green at the end of an almost British fairway running through the dunes.

to a green surrounded by a wasteland of rough-hewn hillocks, pot bunkers and the beach itself immediately to the rear.

The ocean has now been visited for the last time, yet a bit of excitement still remains, for the 471-yard 16th is outstanding. It is just barely a par five but one that requires a drive angled across a wide expanse of Hook pond. As this tee shot is generally played straight downwind, the golfer can achieve a huge amount here – but mishit or miscalculate and five quickly becomes the best-case scenario.

Though somewhat less challenging than in Willie Park's day, the 328-yard 17th remains a gem nonetheless. One final carry across the pond is required on the tee shot, and it allows some opportunity to drive on or very close to the green. The rub, however, is a tiny, angled putting surface

that actually opens up more readily from the safer right side of the fairway and which is both tightly bunkered and closely flanked by intersecting roads (out-of-bounds) just off its back edge. With relative modesty the 378-yard 18th then closes things out, running straight to an ample, heavily bunkered green.

WILLIE PARK'S LEGACY

Though notably short in this era of enhanced equipment, Maidstone relies on the ever-present elements, deep bunkers and thicket-strewn scrub as well as the waters of Hook pond to remain a challenging and distinctively charming course. Olympia Fields has hosted four Major championships, yet Maidstone with its windswept landscape reminiscent of the UK is, for Willie Park Jnr at least, a most appropriate legacy.

The Country Club
Brookline, Massachusetts

Though The Country Club dates back to 1892, golf was not introduced until the following year, when it was played over a rudimentary six holes. These were extended to nine by newly arrived professional Willie Campbell in 1894. That December, the club made history as one of the five founding members of the United States Golf Association (USGA).

The Country Club
Brookline, Massachusetts

Designers: Willie Campbell, 1894 and
William Flynn, 1927
Major events: US Open 1913, 1963, 1988;
US Amateur 1910, 1922, 1934, 1935,
1957, 1982, 2013; US Women's Amateur
1902, 1941, 1995; Ryder Cup 1999;
Walker Cup 1932, 1973

CARD OF THE COURSE

HOLE	YARDS	PAR	HOLE	YARDS	PAR
1.	450	4	10.	447	4
2.	190	3	11.	450	4
3.	451	4	12.	486	4
4.	335	4	13.	436	4
5.	432	4	14.	534	5
6.	310	4	15.	432	4
7.	197	3	16.	186	3
8.	378	4	17.	370	4
9.	513	5	18.	436	4
OUT	3,256	35	IN	3,777	36
			TOTAL	7,033	71

The concept of the modern country club – the full-service, family-oriented facility featuring recreational aspects beyond golf – is largely an American one, its standing as a mark of suburban affluence wielding more impact in the USA than anywhere else. As such, nearly 6,000 American courses use the phrase 'Country Club' within their names. This is a large enough number to give the notion of any single one calling itself The Country Club an apparent touch of arrogance nonpareil. The club in question happens to be The Country Club, situated in the prosperous Boston suburb of Brookline and, not coincidentally, the very first of its type in the entire US – a circumstance under which, admittedly, the name rings more original than haughty.

By the turn of the 20th century, The Country Club golf course had 18 holes (mostly Willie Campbell's), and these ranked among the best of a rather primitive American crop. The club then hosted local hero Francis Ouimet's seminal play-off victory over England's Harry Vardon and Ted Ray at

The composite 11th hole used for US Opens has witnessed some notoriety, particularly when two sevens cost Arnold Palmer the title in the 1963 Open.

the 1913 US Open, before undergoing a substantial renovation (including the addition of a third nine) by another area native, William Flynn, in 1927.

It is essentially this 1927 configuration (with a dash of contemporary paint from Rees Jones) that the members still play today. When US Opens and Ryder Cups come to The Country Club, the par-four 11th is actually a composite hole, cobbled together in a temporary manner from a pair of shorter holes on the club's third nine. Indeed, this entire tournament course is itself a composite, mixing holes from all three nines to create an otherwise-nonexistent championship 18.

From 2007 architect Gil Hanse has carried out a thorough overhaul of the course, its bunkering and, in particular, its tree management. Importantly this has opened up glorious internal views and vistas lost for generations.

A TIMELESS CHAMPIONSHIP TEST

To suggest that a course that retains several 19th-century holes is old-fashioned hardly passes for insight, but The Country Club serves as a particularly illuminating example of early New England architecture, its tiny greens, rock outcroppings and frequent blind shots beautifully

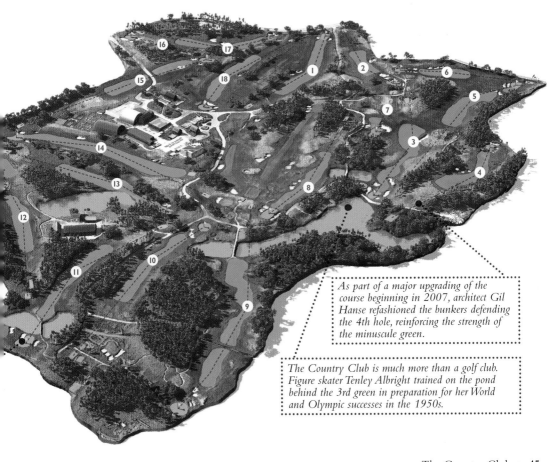

As part of a major upgrading of the course beginning in 2007, architect Gil Hanse refashioned the bunkers defending the 4th hole, reinforcing the strength of the minuscule green.

The Country Club is much more than a golf club. Figure skater Tenley Albright trained on the pond behind the 3rd green in preparation for her World and Olympic successes in the 1950s.

illustrating the natural design style of a less mechanized time. Occupying land where the club's ancient racetrack once sat, the opening two holes are reasonably flat before the topography asserts itself at the 451-yard 3rd, where drives positioned close to a left-side fairway bunker leave an open approach while those played from the right will be blind – unless the shot is long enough to carry an impeding clump of ledge rock, after which only a simple wedge shot remains. The 335-yard 4th is drivable, but its miniscule putting surface is flanked by six bunkers, while the 7th, a 197-yarder to an elevated, wonderfully contoured green, is the only surviving hole from Willie Campbell's 1894 nine.

In the eyes of many, the composite course's best hole is the 513-yard 9th, known colloquially as the Himalayas for its rough-and-tumble terrain. From an elevated tee, the drive is played to a twisting fairway pinched on the right by another encroaching rock formation. To have a chance to reach the green in two, a player must either hit the ball between the rocks and thick left-side woods or attempt to carry the rocks entirely. Either method, if brought off successfully, leaves the golfer with an uphill long-iron to a notably small green behind a series of five bunkers stepped into the hillside. For the 2013 US Amateur this hole was played as a 505-yards par four.

TESTING PAR FOURS

The composite course's back nine begins with a run of four consecutive long and difficult two-shotters. Most notable is the 11th, a 450-yarder requiring a drawn tee shot to a tightly wooded fairway, then a long approach over a pond to a green small enough to serve normally as the putting surface of a 108-yard par three. If possible, the 12th (which regularly plays as the Primrose Course's par-five 8th) is even more difficult, stretching to 486 yards, the latter third of which is

Sound decisions on the tee are needed to attain the 3rd green.

The 17th hole looks benign, but it has been the scene of many triumphs and failures in top level golf at Brookline.

elevated. Here the green is tucked away to the left, leaving any tee ball not placed down the right side of the fairway with an approach at least partially obscured by trees. However the USGA and the club became dissatisfied that driving distance from the tee was compromised because the fairway was interrupted 310 yards from the tee. So a new tee was constructed, making the hole into a 623-yard par five, seen by the world for the first time in the 2013 Amateur. The 436-yard 13th is also not easy, with a right-side lake and the possibility of an awkward downhill lie leading many to lay up with an iron or fairway metal off the tee.

SOME HISTORICAL FINISHERS

The horseshoe-shaped mounding that guards the left side of the fairway at the 534-yard 14th is vintage throwback material, and the hole itself – reachable in two, but featuring an elevated, steeply pitched green – is another of admirable quality. It played as a 508 yard par four in the 2013 Amateur. The 15th, at 432 yards, was a road-crossed two-shotter squeezed between the clubhouse complex and the northern property boundary. A new tee

added in 2011 by Gil Hanse has given an increase in 55 yards in length, playing to the most spacious green on the course. The 186-yard 16th is a fairly basic par three.

The 17th, though only 370 yards, has influenced three US Opens. It was here that Harry Vardon famously drove into a left-side fairway bunker, ending his hopes of capturing the 1913 US Open play-off, and also where Justin Leonard's clinching 45-foot putt sparked the over-the-top celebration that was to mark America's remarkable come-from-behind victory in the 1999 Ryder Cup.

The 436-yard 18th has also seen its share of drama, such as when Curtis Strange's fine up-and-down from the front bunker forced a Monday play-off with Nick Faldo at the 1988 US Open, a contest that Strange ultimately went on to win by four shots. This particular bunker seems a perfect way to finish, too, for its wall-to-wall, essentially penal nature represents one final engaging reminder of the architecture of a bygone day, an era from which The Country Club remains a shining, and still highly challenging, standard-bearer.

Pine Valley
Clementon, New Jersey

Widely ranked the finest course in the world for as long as such ratings have been in vogue, Pine Valley was the brainchild of one man, a Philadelphia hotel owner and fine amateur golfer named George Crump.

Pine Valley Golf Club
Clementon, New Jersey

Designer: George Crump, 1915
Major events: Walker Cup 1936, 1985

'You love it, and you hate it. It's beautiful and it's horrible. It's wonderful, and yet it's just so darn difficult.'
JAY SIGEL, DISTINGUISHED AMATEUR GOLFER AND WALKER CUP CAPTAIN

Yet while Crump located this matchless site among the southern New Jersey pine trees, and bore primary responsibility for its design, he also called upon the services of a number of distinguished Golden-Age architects to aid in its planning.

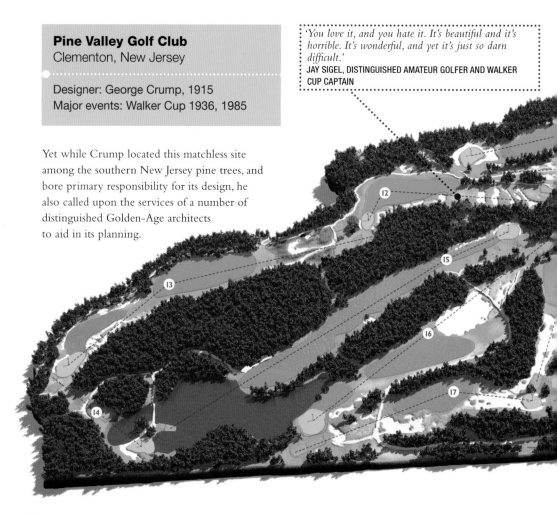

AN ARCHITECTURAL DREAM TEAM

Initially there was Walter Travis, America's first genuinely great player (and later a prolific course designer) from whom Crump solicited suggestions. Far more involved was the eminent British architect Harry Colt, who, according to four-time US Amateur champion and Crump friend Jerome Travers, was engaged 'to come to this country to plan a course of surpassing merit and extraordinary beauty'. Colt, Travers explained, 'pitched his tent in the woods and camped there for a week or more.

CARD OF THE COURSE

HOLE	YARDS	PAR	HOLE	YARDS	PAR
1.	421	4	10.	161	3
2.	368	4	11.	397	4
3.	198	3	12.	337	4
4.	451	4	13.	486	4
5.	235	3	14.	220	3
6.	387	4	15.	615	5
7.	636	5	16.	475	4
8.	326	4	17.	345	4
9.	459	4	18.	483	4
OUT	3,481	35	IN	3,519	35
			TOTAL	7,000	70

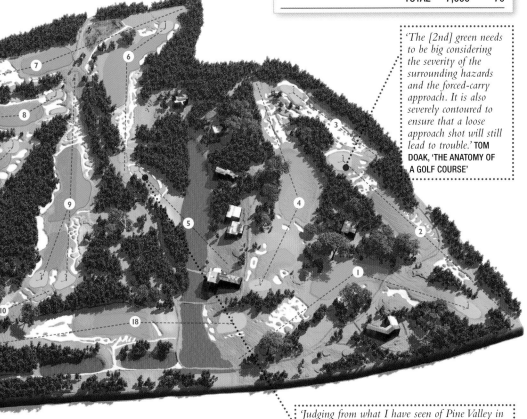

'The [2nd] green needs to be big considering the severity of the surrounding hazards and the forced-carry approach. It is also severely contoured to ensure that a loose approach shot will still lead to trouble.' **TOM DOAK, 'THE ANATOMY OF A GOLF COURSE'**

'Judging from what I have seen of Pine Valley in its early stages ... it will be the greatest course in America'.
CHARLES BLAIR MACDONALD

The 483-yard 18th is a mammoth finisher that requires an intimidating carry over typical Pine Valley terrain off the tee.

He emerged from his hibernation enthralled.' This enthralment led to the production of an 18-hole plan, aspects of which – but only aspects – appeared in Crump's eventual finished product.

When it was time to build, George Crump himself directed Pine Valley's construction in a painstaking, hole-by-hole process. For five years he lived as a semi-recluse, residing in the woods with only his hunting dogs for company, and on his untimely death in 1918 four holes (today's 12th–15th) remained unfinished. In due course Crump's plans for this final quartet were brought to life by Merion-designer Hugh Wilson and his brother Alan, apparently with suggestions from Colt's esteemed partner Charles Alison.

Alison also provided additional renovative ideas to the finished course, while other noted designers to offer their services included William Flynn (early construction work and minor 1929 renovations), George Thomas (in support of William Flynn), Perry Maxwell (several green rebuilds/alterations) and A. W. Tillinghast (sundry thoughts, little documented).

A PRIVATE RETREAT

Pine Valley is situated on land described by Jerome Travers as 'neither flat nor hilly', and resembling 'a desert into which have been dropped clusters of beautiful trees'. But those 'clusters' have grown, for today's layout features none of the open vistas of yesteryear, with each hole now hemmed in almost entirely by woods. The course itself has long been viewed as an unbeatable monster, the world's hardest inland layout, and stories of astonishingly high scores (such as Bobby Jones's 88 on his first visit) abound. But while it certainly is difficult – as a USGA slope of 155 on a 7,000-yard layout conclusively attests – assertions that it is a purely penal house of horrors miss the mark widely.

Most of Pine Valley's fairways are generously wide, its greens usually present ample targets, and with six par fours under 400 yards, it is hardly backbreaking. There are, perhaps, more death-or-glory shots here than on any other golf course. Pine Valley also presents numerous strategic challenges within its rigours, the 6th, 7th, 13th and 16th being highly thought-provoking tests.

The 1st, a sharp dogleg right, is a fairly stout opener, but the challenge really picks up at the 2nd – one of golf's epic drive-and-pitches. Here the golfer must carry 150 yards of sandy scrub just to reach a fairway that, though only 30 yards wide, should not be missed with a long-iron or fairway metal. What remains is frightening: little more than a wedge shot, but one played sharply uphill to a massive green behind a steep wall of sand and deep grass.

MEMORABLE PAR THREES
Pine Valley features an exceptional set of par threes, beginning with the downhill 3rd, whose heavily contoured, sand-ringed putting surface offers several very demanding pin placements. The 5th is a 235-yarder of worldwide renown. Crump intended to make this a relatively short hole played to a waterside green, but this plan was scrapped when Harry Colt suggested shelving the putting surface upon a distant hillside. The result was an uphill hole of almost singular difficulty, with a long carry required to reach a narrow ribbon of fairway or, ideally, the smallish, back-to-front sloping green.

Doglegging sharply right around a scrub-filled valley, the 6th dares the player to make the 230-yard carry across the corner, because this leaves a short, unimpeded pitch straight up the green. The farther the drive moves leftwards the more a large greenside bunker impedes play.

'HELL'S HALF ACRE'
The recently lengthened 636-yard 7th has long been known as 'Hell's half acre' in celebration of the 100-yard long sandy waste area that crosses the fairway some 330 yards off the tee. An inadequate tee shot very likely results in a forced lay up on the second shot, the hole culminating in a putting surface that is nearly an island within even more sandy waste.

Things get shorter, but in no way easier, at the 8th – a remarkably dangerous hole that Bernard Darwin once observed places 'no limit on the player's liabilities'. A tougher drive-and-pitch would be difficult to imagine, though the nature of the challenge is simple and clearly defined.

The 10th is virtually surrounded by sand, though its primary hazard, a tiny, especially nasty pot bunker, actually evolved naturally and was not part of Crump's original design.

A MODERN EXPANSION
One of the game's celebrated par fours, the 486-yard 13th, has as its central feature a green angled off to the left, behind a large patch of scrub and slightly encroaching trees. The challenge has long been to hit the uphill tee shot far enough to make attempting this hazardous crossing viable, the alternative being a safe lay-up to the right with hopes of getting up and down for four. Also newly lengthened is the 220-yard 14th – a hole of real beauty played downhill across a lake to a flattish, sand-ringed green.

The 615-yard 15th is a brute, beginning with a 115-yard forced carry over the lake, then sweeping uphill to a distant green. Central to this hole's challenge is the fact that it narrows progressively as it goes, calling into question the value of blasting a second close when the lay-up area some 125 yards short is infinitely safer.

Even greater thought is required on the 475-yard 16th, its 85-yard wide fairway angling left-to-right beyond a vast expanse of sand. Ahead, the huge green has water on its right, with trees and sand creeping in from the left, making a wonderfully strategic hole. Finally the 483-yard 18th is a punishing par four where the recent addition of 60 yards has reintroduced much of the challenge that once defined this impressive finisher.

Merion
Ardmore, Pennsylvania

There has long been a certain cachet associated with golf's true amateur course designers, men who, with little prior background, ventured into the field to build just a handful of courses – in some cases, perhaps even just one – such as Hugh Wilson at Merion.

Merion Golf Club (East course)
Ardmore, Pennsylvania

Designer: Hugh Wilson, 1912
Major events: US Open 1934,
1950, 1971, 1981, 2013;
US Amateur 1916, 1924,
1930, 1966, 1989, 2005;
Walker Cup 2009;
US Women's Amateur
1904, 1909, 1926,
1949; Curtis Cup 1954

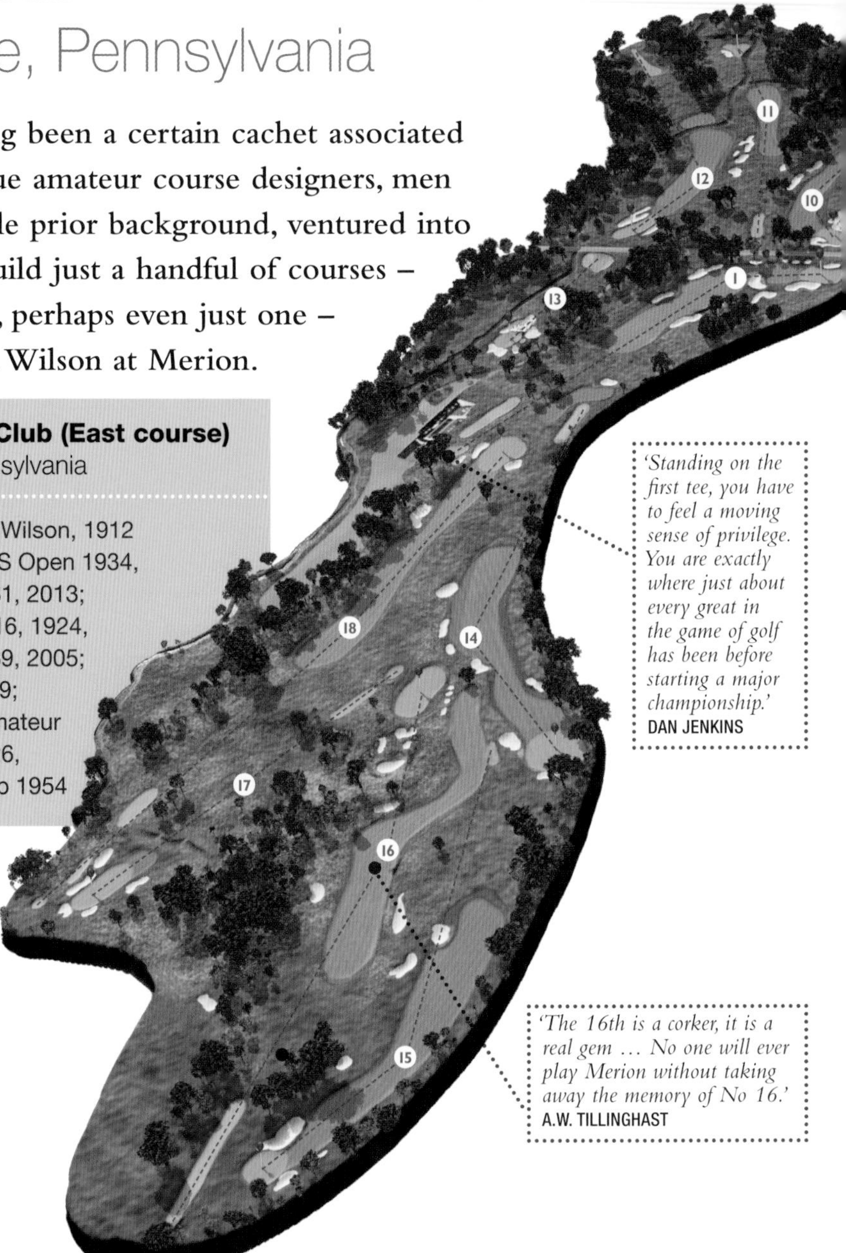

'Standing on the first tee, you have to feel a moving sense of privilege. You are exactly where just about every great in the game of golf has been before starting a major championship.'
DAN JENKINS

'The 16th is a corker, it is a real gem ... No one will ever play Merion without taking away the memory of No 16.'
A.W. TILLINGHAST

Theoretically, with a limited body of work, the concepts of amateur course designers are fresh, their efforts focused exclusively on the legacy-building task at hand. There are no issues of being spread too thinly or recycling a previous entry from some grand catalogue of past work. Evidence in support of this theory is plentiful: George Crump exemplified it at Pine Valley, as did Henry and William Fownes at Oakmont and, to a large extent, Bobby Jones at Augusta National and Jack Neville and Douglas Grant at Pebble Beach. To this list must be added perhaps the pre-eminent example of first-time golf design greatness: Hugh Wilson at Merion.

STUDYING ABROAD

A former Princeton golf team captain and a good Philadelphia-area amateur, Wilson was appointed in 1910 to lead the then Merion Cricket Club's committee in charge of building a new golf course. To prepare, the committee sent him on an extended trip to the British Isles to study the world's great layouts, stopping en route in Southampton, New York to meet America's course design pioneer, Charles Blair Macdonald. Wilson ultimately returned to Philadelphia armed with piles of notes and sketches of the UK's finest holes and, with apparent continuing advice from Macdonald, went to work.

CARD OF THE COURSE

HOLE	YARDS	PAR	HOLE	YARDS	PAR
1.	350	4	10.	303	4
2	556	5	11.	367	4
3.	256	3	12.	403	4
4.	628	5	13.	115	3
5.	504	4	14.	464	4
6.	487	4	15.	411	4
7.	360	4	16.	430	4
8.	359	4	17.	246	3
9.	236	3	18.	521	4
OUT	**3,736**	**36**	**IN**	**3,260**	**34**
			TOTAL	**6,996**	**70**

The site of Merion's East Course was a compact L-shaped tract that held the remains of two farms, as well as an abandoned rock quarry. Working with a construction crew that included future Golden-Age designer William Flynn, Flynn's eventual partner Howard Toomey and future long-serving Merion greenkeeper Joe Valentine, Wilson formulated a 6,235-yard layout that laid the foundation for that in play today.

Significant change would first come in 1922 when the 10th, 11th and 12th holes were reconfigured to avoid crossing Ardmore Avenue. Wilson planned to upgrade things by performing a 1925 overhaul of the course's bunkering, but died of pneumonia before its completion.

The project was continued by Flynn, Toomey and Valentine, who famously spread bedsheets in the locations of proposed hazards to gauge their visual impact before building them, a technique that resulted in bunkers widely rated among the game's most strategic and attractive. Finally, in 1929, the 1st fairway was moved farther away from the adjacent Golf House Road and that, except for some minor nips and tucks and a little recent lengthening, finalized the Merion layout.

RICH CHAMPIONSHIP HISTORY

Merion was widely considered a truly modern course, quickly establishing itself among America's finest tournament venues, eventually hosting two of the defining events in golf history. In 1930, the club witnessed Bobby Jones's peerless victory at the US Amateur. Exactly 20 years later it was Ben Hogan's turn to achieve a miracle, returning from a near-fatal car accident to capture his second US Open.

A FAST GETAWAY

The course begins in measured but eminently stylish fashion, as the 1st doglegs gently right, its boundaries flanked by no fewer than 13 bunkers. With the entire right side of its narrow fairway

The first encounter with the quarry: the approach to the 430-yard 16th. A narrow lay-up area exists well to the right.

flanked by an out-of-bounds the 2nd is somewhat stiffer, while the 256-yard 3rd plays slightly uphill and across a swale, its elevated, left-to-right sloping green protected by a particularly dangerous bunker short-right. The brook-fronted 4th may occasionally be reachable in two nowadays, and provides what amounts to a third birdie opportunity in the first four holes, although no eagles were recorded in the 2013 US Open.

THE HEROIC FIFTH

Strokes gained early may be repaid at the demanding 5th. Featuring a new US Open-friendly tee, it is a wonderfully natural test with fairway and green sloping noticeably towards the stream that flanks the hole's entire left side. The challenge here is to drive as close to this as possible, for tee shots bailed out to the right leave a long-iron second from a hook lie to a green running towards the immediately adjacent stream. Driving at the 6th, the ideal angle of approach lies along the fairway's right side, but to reach it requires a faded tee shot skirting dangerously close to out-of-bounds.

Ending the front nine the 9th, plays slightly downhill to a large, right-to-left curving green. While the putting surface is behind a pond and flanked well right by a creek, a greater challenge lies in the five bunkers that guard its sides and rear.

A PROCESSION OF FAMOUS HOLES

A short two-shotter, the renowned 11th plays to a pear-shaped green wedged into the semicircular curve of Cobb's Creek, which also crosses the fairway at approximately 275 yards. The tee shot must be a lay-up – disappointing in a strategic sense, yet also a guarantee that today's players face the same death-defying pitch that challenged Bobby Jones.

With the other par threes all measuring at least 200 yards, the 115-yard 13th is by far Merion's shortest hole, but its small, bowl-like putting surface is ringed by five bunkers, the largest of which, sitting directly front and centre, is dotted by clumps of dune grass. This has long ranked among America's vaunted short part threes.

In 2013 holes 14 and 15 demonstrated their high quality being rated the fifth and third hardest on the course respectively.

THE QUARRY HOLES

Most who find the fairway on the 16th play their second across the quarry to a two-tiered green sloping heavily from back to front, but for club golfers a bail-out area on the right is maintained.

Recently stretched into a 246-yard monster playing from an elevated tee back across the quarry is the par-three 17th. While the carry is significant, better players are bothered less by the quarry and more by the green complex, for the putting surface is narrow and sloping left to right, and is flanked on three sides by sand.

Finally the 521-yard, par-four 18th, proved the hardest hole during the 2013 Open. A compulsory carry over the quarry must reach a narrowing fairway with trees and out-of-bounds flanking its left side. The second shot, generally played off a downhill lie, then requires a long-iron to a shallow green positioned atop an upslope, and guarded left and right by sand.

Measuring only 6,482 yards during the 1981 US Open, Merion was long viewed as distinctly short by postwar championship standards. Its recent lengthening has stretched it to just under 7,000 yards. Yet Merion remains one of America's most traditional courses, exemplified by the club's long-time trademark: wicker baskets perched atop the flagsticks.

Oakmont
Oakmont, Pennsylvania

It is not entirely certain when it was decided that Oakmont should be the toughest golf course in America, nor whether such a decision was made by the club's founder, Henry Fownes, or the man who played the largest role in shaping its present layout, Henry's son, William.

Oakmont Country Club
Oakmont, Pennsylvania

Designers: Henry Fownes and William Fownes, 1904
Major events: US Open 1927, 1935, 1953, 1962, 1973, 1983, 1994, 2007; US Amateur 1919, 1925, 1938, 1969, 2003; USPGA 1922, 1951, 1978; US Women's Open 1992; Curtis Cup 1986

As generations of golfers can attest, if Oakmont is not *the* toughest American golf course, it surely doesn't miss by much. Oakmont was the brainchild of Henry Fownes, a steel industry tycoon in turn-of-the-century Pittsburgh. An avid and capable golfer, Fownes decided in 1903 to build his own club. Purchasing 200 acres of rolling, open farmland south of the Allegheny river, he staked out his course that autumn, opening for play in spring 1904. This initial layout was sparsely bunkered and not particularly difficult, but cognizant of the liveliness of the new Haskell ball,

CARD OF THE COURSE

HOLE	YARDS	PAR	HOLE	YARDS	PAR
1.	482	4	10.	435	4
2.	341	4	11.	379	4
3.	428	4	12.	667	5
4.	609	5	13.	183	3
5.	382	4	14.	358	4
6.	194	3	15.	500	4
7.	479	4	16.	231	3
8.	288	3	17.	313	4
9.	477	5	18.	484	4
OUT	**3,680**	**35**	**IN**	**3,550**	**35**
			TOTAL	**7,230**	**70**

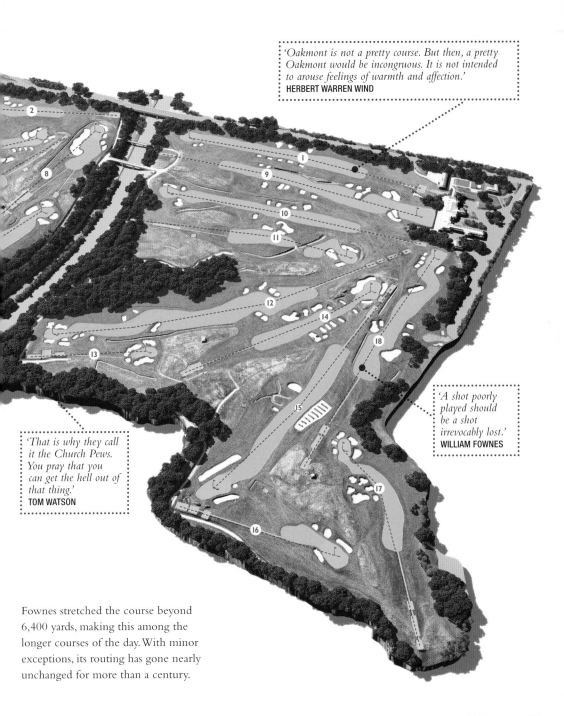

'Oakmont is not a pretty course. But then, a pretty Oakmont would be incongruous. It is not intended to arouse feelings of warmth and affection.'
HERBERT WARREN WIND

'A shot poorly played should be a shot irrevocably lost.'
WILLIAM FOWNES

'That is why they call it the Church Pews. You pray that you can get the hell out of that thing.'
TOM WATSON

Fownes stretched the course beyond 6,400 yards, making this among the longer courses of the day. With minor exceptions, its routing has gone nearly unchanged for more than a century.

FATHER-AND-SON TEAM

Henry's son William was the 1910 US Amateur champion, twice a Walker Cup participant and president of the USGA in 1926 and '27. Such honours added credibility to his inheritance of the Oakmont mantle, and while some question remains as to precisely who was in charge of the course design it is generally believed that William was the man most responsible for the golf course's metamorphosis into a man-eating monster.

With the help of the club's long-serving professional/superintendent Emil 'Dutch' Loeffler, the revamping by William Fownes began in the early 1920s and included the addition of numerous bunkers, the rebuilding of greens, some inevitable lengthening and the construction of a new 16th hole. The club also enhanced its reputation for being hell-bent on difficulty by beginning a four-decade practice of furrowing its bunkers – using a specially designed rake to create golf-ball-wide grooves in the sand that, when drawn at 90-degree angles to the target line, make anything more than a rudimentary blast virtually impossible.

REGULAR HOST TO MAJORS

A course of such renowned difficulty appeals to the USGA and the 2007 US Open represented an unprecedented eighth time this championship has visited Oakmont. The club has further hosted five US Amateurs, three PGA championships and a US Women's Open. Tommy Armour, Sam Parks, Ben Hogan, Jack Nicklaus, Johnny Miller, Larry Nelson, Ernie Els and Angel Cabrera make an impressive list of Open champions. The closing 63 that clinched Johnny Miller's 1973 title may well be the greatest round of tournament golf ever played.

DISTINCTIVE GREENS

The present Oakmont layout is greatly expanded from Henry Fownes's day, its 7,230-yard US Open set-up representing an especially long test with par reduced to 70. Despite featuring five Open par fours in excess of 460 yards, of far greater concern to the professional are the layout's more than 175 bunkers in addition to some of the nastiest rough imaginable. Its greens, a set of utterly special putting surfaces, are unmatched for their mix of size, firmness, speed and contour. Despite its reputation for unadulterated difficulty Oakmont also offers a number of strategically excellent holes.

Immediately the golfer faces one of the game's hardest openers – a 482-yard par four played downhill to a putting surface that falls dangerously away from front to back. The 2nd is frequently played with a long-iron or fairway metal, followed by a short pitch. The problem is that, with the green slanting toward ten o'clock, the tee ball must flirt with a cluster of six right-side bunkers, plus a single newer hazard added mid-fairway, to gain the optimum angle of approach.

THE CHURCH PEWS

The 3rd is memorable for its famed Church Pews, a 120-yard long left-side bunker broken by a dozen nearly symmetrical grass ridges. One of golf's more original and striking hazards, it frequently requires escapes to be sideways pitches. Even from the fairway the approach is testing: the green is perched on a large knob, dictating delicate bump-and-run recoveries for shots missed short or slightly long.

Oakmont's challenge resumes sternly at the 479-yard 7th, followed by the long one-shot 8th, which garnered a great deal of 2007 attention for a new US Open tee measuring 288 yards. With its green curving leftwards around a massive bunker, this oversized par three was originally designed to be played with a driver, measuring 253 yards for the 1927 US Open.

Rear view of the dangerous 484-yard 18th, where even the world's best are generally happy with pars.

The 477-yard 9th is a sporting par five for club members but is played as a monstrous two-shotter by the professionals. Central to its challenge is a blind tee shot to a fairway whose left edge is menaced by one of several man-made ditches (staked as lateral water hazards) that appear throughout the property. The approach is then played between multiple bunkers to a nastily rippled putting surface that, at 20,000 square feet, actually doubles as the club's practice green. However, the 435-yard 10th is statistically even harder, its downhill approach somewhat resembling that encountered on the 1st hole, complete with sloping putting surface. All told, any golfer achieving par figures from the 7th through the 10th may well pick up more than a single stroke against the field. Normally a 602-yard test, the 12th was extended to an unprecedented 667 yards for the 2007 Open.

POWERHOUSE FINISHERS

Oakmont's suitably big finish begins with the famous 15th, a long par four now played from a 500-yard tee. With a second set of Church

Pews on the favoured left side and with sand and multiple ditches to the right, this blind tee shot may be the toughest on the course.

The 231-yard 16th is another stiff test, requiring a well-struck long-iron to finish anywhere near the pin, particularly when it is cut back-right. On the other hand the 17th is an incongruously short but intriguing two-shotter played to a narrow green behind a huge, 12-foot deep bunker. Despite running steadily uphill, this 313-yarder is readily drivable by the modern professional, provided he is first able to carry a set of six left-side fairway bunkers, then run the ball between the aforementioned front bunker and a rough-laden bank creeping in from the left.

Oakmont closes with a dangerous par four measuring 484 yards, its challenge lying not just in avoiding a left-side ditch and five bunkers and but also in holding anything but a well-struck draw in its narrow, left-to-right sloping fairway. The approach is then slightly uphill to a green filled with enough pitches and rolls to make even short-iron approaches extremely difficult to stop close to the hole.

South-eastern states

Although the first recorded golf clubs in America existed, temporarily, in Charleston, South Carolina and Savannah, Georgia during the 1740s, the modern game of golf was slower to take root in the south-east, largely due to pre-1930s difficulties in consistently growing high-calibre turf grass amid the heat and humidity.

As the game reappeared in the south-eastern states towards the end of the 19th century, it was essentially in a rudimentary, sand-green form, located in areas catering primarily to seasonal resort guests. Agronomical advances have long since replaced the sand greens – and even, to some extent, the nasty grain inherent in their primary replacement, Bermuda grass – while more than a

century later resorts remain a leading component of south-eastern golf, with a healthy number of real-estate development courses thrown in.

Traditional private clubs – those not built around the selling of houses – have always existed in the region, and so long as the wealthy desire less crowded, more secluded places to play, they always will. But with land acquisition and course

Ballyhack in Roanoake, Virginia, a masterful contemporary layout by Lester George making full use of the majestic landscape.

WEST VIRGINIA

The Homestead (Cascades Course)
page 66

3 ▸

4 ▸ VIRGINIA

Ballyhack

NORTH CAROLINA

5 ▸

Asheville

Pinehurst (No 2 Course)
page 70

KENTUCKY

TENNESSEE

● Camden

KANSAS

SOUTH CAROLINA ● Myrtle Beach

● Aiken

Augusta National
page 78

MISSISSIPPI ALABAMA GEORGIA

● Kiawah Island
Harbour Town
page 74

Hilton Head

OUISIANA

● Georgia Coastal Islands

● Jacksonville

TPC at Sawgrass
page 84

St Augustine

FLORIDA

7 ▸ ● Orlando

8 ▸

Seminole
page 88

● Hobe Sound
● Palm Beach
● Boca Raton
● Fort Lauderdale

1 ▸

Fort Myers

6 ▸ ● Miami

● Naples

2 ▸

Biscayne Bay

construction costs climbing ever higher, real estate has become a necessary component to many a course development plan – and the idea is hardly a new one. In 1926, Sarasota – Florida's Sara Bay Country Club[1] (then called Whitfield Estates) – began selling plots around its Donald Ross-designed course with no less than Bobby Jones leading a team of 'salesmen' that included Jim Barnes, Johnny Farrell, the Briton Archie Compston and the French star Arnaud Massey. Indeed, while Florida's grandest course, the Seminole Golf Club, was built residence-free, even Miami's Indian Creek[2] – an ultra-exclusive Golden Age club situated on a private island in Biscayne Bay – was laid out with a row of expensive plots for houses lining its perimeter, remaining ultra expensive today.

MOUNTAIN RETREATS

Before the real-estate projects, however, there were resorts, the earliest being located primarily in mountain regions where rich city dwellers travelled to escape the summer heat. Among the very earliest were The Homestead[3] (1766) and The Greenbrier[4] (1778), a pair of stately 18th-century Blue Ridge establishments straddling the Virginia–West Virginia state line. The Homestead, in particular, was a ground-breaker, with its first six holes of golf opening in 1892, even though the game had been played near The Greenbrier in 1884 at the Oakhurst Links. This short-lived (but later restored) nine remains America's oldest still-active golf club, but the resort itself did not really get involved in golf until the building of Charles Blair Macdonald's Old

The Greenbrier at White Sulphur Springs, West Virginia is a vast estate offering full resort facilities, including three golf courses.

The five courses at Doral are now part of the Trump Collection, with the Blue Monster course undergoing redesign by Gil Hanse.

White Course in 1914. Today both facilities remain world-class destinations, each featuring 54 holes of golf with The Homestead's Cascades Course being among the nation's very best.

Another early resort centre was Pinehurst, initially a health-oriented retreat in the sand-hills region of south–central North Carolina that, by 1898, was embracing the game of golf. In 1900 the resort hired Donald Ross to be its winter professional and, within a few years, the transplanted Scot's architectural prowess had turned Pinehurst into the self-proclaimed 'St Andrews of America'. Today the resort's eight courses serve as the hub of the sand-hills golf explosion, with well over 30 area layouts catering to public, resort and private golfers alike. Pinehurst's famous No 2 course remains the centrepiece, although its No 4 and No 8 courses, plus nearby Pine Needles[5] (a three-time US Women's Open site) are also worthy of note.

DOMINANCE BY FLORIDA

Numerous other resorts also drew early golfers to the region, with places such as Camden and Aiken (South Carolina), Asheville (North Carolina), Augusta National and the coastal islands of Georgia, and the Mississippi gulf coast all appearing prominently on any period golfing map. But by the onset of the Depression in the early 1930s, the giant of south-eastern golf was – as it remains today – Florida.

Once upon a time the Sunshine State's golf centres sprang up along pioneering 19th-century railway lines built by men such as Henry Flagler and Henry Plant, with Miami, Palm Beach and St Augustine the first major destinations. In the postwar era, however, agronomical advances, the widespread advent of air conditioning and a more affluent society sparked a second boom, with Doral[6], Disney World[7] and Innisbrook[8] leading the game farther inland, where vast quantities of

Pete Dye's Ocean Course at Kiawah Island had been awarded the 1991 Ryder Cup matches even before it was completed.

inexpensive land suitable for golf could still be secured.

Resorts continued to be built right into the new millennium, though by the 1970s the broader body of course construction had moved into residential club development, particularly on the south-eastern coast where large golf-oriented communities began eating up massive chunks of real estate. Today Boca Raton heads a boom that has created a veritable golfing greenbelt from Fort Lauderdale all the way north to ultra-affluent Hobe Sound, with the more inland facilities often encroaching on the everglades – sites that would have been deemed unsuitable for development

(based on heat and a lack of verifiable terra firma) until the 1950s. Orlando, the coastal region south of Jacksonville (led by Pete Dye's landmark Tournament Players' Club at Sawgrass) and much of outlying Fort Myers have also expanded considerably, but the heavyweight champion of contemporary Florida golf growth is certainly Naples, which since the early 1990s has come to hold its own with any of America's golfing addresses.

All told, Florida today offers more than 70 prominent resorts (many featuring multiple courses) and more than 450 private clubs (the vast majority tied to real-estate developments)

– though almost all are hampered by the state's pancake-flat landscape, which makes the over-use of water, sand and palpably unnatural mounding a frequent design issue.

ECONOMIC SIGNIFICANCE OF GOLF

Such large-scale postwar development has hardly been confined to Florida, for in South Carolina major coastal areas, particularly Hilton Head and Kiawah islands and Myrtle Beach, largely define south-eastern contemporary golf, drawing tourists and seasonal residents from across the nation. Hilton Head offers more than 45 courses on-island or in its immediate environs, highlighted by Pete Dye's seminal Harbour Town Golf Links. Kiawah is both newer and smaller, but several of its seven layouts rate highly, chiefly Dye's spectacular Ocean Course, site of the highly competitive 1991 Ryder Cup. Myrtle Beach, on the other hand, represents mass-produced resort golf at its grandest, with more than 120 area courses serving as a clear demonstration of golf's huge importance to the economy of the entire south-eastern region.

Mid Pines in the North Carolina sandhills is a Donald Ross gem from 1920, sensitively restored by Kyle Franz in 2013.

Cascades
Hot Springs, Virginia

Although it lies mostly along a valley floor, the Cascades has long been known as America's 'best mountain golf course' for a reason, requiring William Flynn to go to extraordinary lengths in his task of building a masterpiece.

The Homestead (Cascades Course)
Hot Springs, Virginia

Designer: William Flynn, 1923
Major events: US Women's Open 1967;
US Amateur 1988; US Women's Amateur
1928; Curtis Cup 1966

'The Cascades' greens seem to confuse newcomers not familiar with mountain courses' irregular horizons as a reference for lining up putts.'
BILL CAMPBELL, FORMER US AMATEUR CHAMPION AND WALKER CUP CAPTAIN

Many are the American resorts that predate the Golden Age of golf design or, for that matter, the modern game's 19th-century US birth altogether. Indeed, a small collection of these timeless getaways have actually existed since before the American Civil War (1861–65). But a resort that predates America itself – the actual formation of the country – well, that is another matter entirely. But such is precisely the case at The Homestead in Hot Springs, Virginia, where the discovery of mineral springs led to the construction of the resort's first accommodation fully ten years prior to the Declaration of Independence, in 1766.

Decade after decade, golfers keep coming back to figure out how to play The Cascades. Surely, this is the greatest compliment an architect and a course can receive?'
RAN MORRISSETT

SINCE 1892

The modern conception of The Homestead, however, really came into being under the ownership of legendary financier J.P. Morgan, who masterminded the expansion in the 1890s that created some of the older buildings still in use today. Golf, for its part, arrived in 1892 in the form of a rudimentary six-hole layout. This course was eventually extended to 18 by Donald Ross in 1913, though its original first tee was incorporated into the new design, making it the oldest continually used opening tee in America.

The Cascades Course came a decade later, after golf's booming popularity threatened to overwhelm the Ross layout entirely. But logistically there were problems, because The Homestead, like most of America's great mountain resorts, is situated in a valley, its golf course occupying reasonably flat land along the floor, with the surrounding hills serving mostly as a wonderfully scenic backdrop. By the early 1920s, there was no further usable land close to the hotel, forcing the consideration of an alternative tract in the nearby village of Healing Springs. Initially, no less than Seth Raynor and A.W. Tillinghast pronounced this site too mountainous to develop, verdicts that might have settled the issue. But a young William Flynn begged to differ, and with his more optimistic assessment managed to land himself – despite little national reputation – a

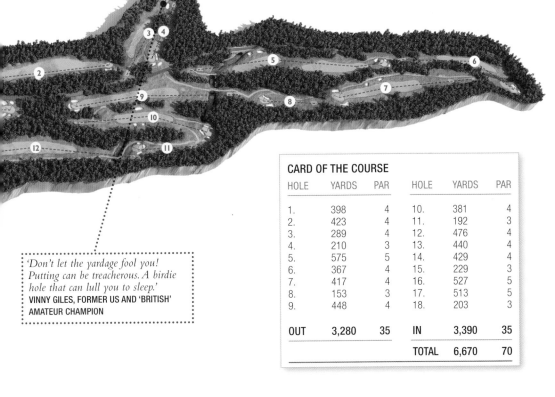

> *'Don't let the yardage fool you! Putting can be treacherous. A birdie hole that can lull you to sleep.'*
> **VINNY GILES, FORMER US AND 'BRITISH' AMATEUR CHAMPION**

CARD OF THE COURSE

HOLE	YARDS	PAR	HOLE	YARDS	PAR
1.	398	4	10.	381	4
2.	423	4	11.	192	3
3.	289	4	12.	476	4
4.	210	3	13.	440	4
5.	575	5	14.	429	4
6.	367	4	15.	229	3
7.	417	4	16.	527	5
8.	153	3	17.	513	5
9.	448	4	18.	203	3
OUT	3,280	35	IN	3,390	35
			TOTAL	6,670	70

very high-profile design commission indeed. Not only were trees cleared and unsuitable terrain dynamited, but the waters of the Swift Run, which meaningfully affects play on six holes, were actually re-routed in several places. It was a monumental task indeed, and though looking remarkably natural given the work performed, there was still more to be done, for Flynn continued tinkering with the Cascades right up until his death in 1945.

In 1934 The Homestead hired an unknown local named Sam Snead to serve as its golf professional. Within three years, Snead was making his living on the PGA Tour, but he never moved far from his roots, retaining an affiliation with either The Homestead or the nearby Greenbrier right up until his death in 2002.

OVER HILLY TERRAIN

The layout's front side becomes more hilly and wooded as it extends south-westwards into a narrow section of the valley, while the back opens up somewhat and is flatter. The outward half features a good early run in the form of three holes wedged into tougher land to the east of Route 220, beginning at the 423-yard 2nd. Here, a heavily drawn tee ball is needed to offset the sharp left-to-right slope of the fairway, while the 289-yard 3rd requires careful planning because a rough-filled gully lies in front of the shallow, elevated green. Attempting to drive to the putting surface seems a low percentage play, but then not many golfers find their blood racing at the prospect of laying up with a 3-iron. The demands are much clearer at the 210-yard, downhill 4th, a Redan-like one-shotter with a green angled right-to-left behind a bunker, a steep drop-off to its rear.

The next four holes – the 575-yard, semiblind 5th, the 367-yard 6th, the uphill 417-yard 7th and tiny 153-yard 8th – do an impressively engineered out-and-back over occasionally tumultuous ground, setting the stage for the demanding

The 16th at Cascades challenges the player's vanity, asking them whether or not to risk carrying the green-front stream.

The first short hole at Cascades is the 210-yard 4th. To miss left, right or long can damage the card early in the round.

par-four 9th. Measuring 448 yards from a tee positioned deep in a chute of trees, this brute requires a nearly 260-yard drive to carry first a deep ravine, then the crest of a steep rise in the fairway, leaving a long second (likely at least to be partially blind) to a green bunkered both left and right.

AN IMPOSING BACK NINE

The back nine has few weak holes and is particularly noteworthy from the 12th through to the 17th. At 476 yards, the 12th is easily the Cascade's longest par four and very likely its toughest, its elevated tee looking down on a fairway pinched right by a thickly wooded hillside and left by the Swift Run. From the fairway, a line of cross-bunkers 80 yards in front of the putting surface shouldn't present a problem, but finding the narrow, tightly bunkered green certainly is. The creek then accompanies the 440-yard 13th northwards, guarding the inside of this downhill dogleg-left two-shotter. If slightly less interesting, the 429-yard

14th and stiff 229-yard 15th are both strong tests, setting the stage for the back-to-back par fives, which are the Cascades's centrepiece.

A genuine classic, the 527-yard 16th doglegs right around a cluster of three bunkers that longer hitters will surely attempt to carry. Then comes the big decision: whether to lay up with a mid-iron or have a go at the putting surface, which is behind a pond and backed by bunkers – a decision made trickier by the green sitting only inches above the waterline, resulting in a not-so-clearly defined target. The 513-yard 17th then bends sharply left, with a small creek catching any drives that skip through the fairway. The approach is then played to another pond-guarded green, though this time a narrow corridor of left-side fairway allows some possibility of running a well- struck ball onto the putting surface. Following these fine three-shotters, the 203-yard 18th may feel a bit anti-climactic, but some allowance had to be made in order to site its illustrious predecessors in their ideal spots.

Pinehurst No 2
Pinehurst, North Carolina

The arrival in the United States in 1899 of a man who appreciated how the game was played in the United Kingdom helped golf gain a foothold in many places there. For instance, pre-1900 the Pinehurst course was rudimentary and of no strategic interest. However, Donald Ross changed all that, with the result that Pinehurst is now often seen as the home of American golf.

Pinehurst Resort (No 2 course)
Pinehurst, North Carolina

Designer: Donald Ross, 1908
Major events: USPGA 1936; Ryder Cup 1951; US Amateur 1962, 2008; US Women's Amateur 1989; US Open 1999, 2005, 2014; US Women's Open 2014

Initially, James Walker Tufts, the resort's owner, hired Donald Ross as the head golf professional, and his duties were club-making and giving lessons. However, within two years, Ross had adjusted to the Bermuda grass and the sand greens and was keen to improve the golf offerings at Pinehurst. Being used to links courses in his native Scotland, Ross was struck by the opportunity that the soil provided in the sand hills of North Carolina. He wrote: 'Only in sandy soil will the drainage problem permit construction of the rolling contours and hollows natural to Scotch seaside courses where golf was born.'

'I sincerely believe this course to be the fairest test of championship golf that I have ever designed.'
DONALD ROSS

'The areas off the greens are masterpieces. I don't think there's anything like it in North America.'
BEN CRENSHAW

THE BUILDING OF MORE COURSES

By 1903, golf at Pinehurst consisted of Pinehurst No 1 and a nine-hole course called No 2. To keep up with golf's growing stature in the United States, the Tufts family asked Ross to redesign Nos 1 and 2 and build courses 3 and 4. Despite four courses, the game was so popular by the early 1920s that the resort was turning away almost 20,000 golfers during its seven-month playing season (prior to air conditioning, the town of Pinehurst emptied during the hot summer months). Further high-quality Ross designs followed in the surrounding

CARD OF THE COURSE

HOLE	YARDS	PAR	HOLE	YARDS	PAR
1.	404	4	10.	607	5
2.	469	4	11.	476	4
3.	336	4	12.	449	4
4.	565	5	13.	378	4
5.	472	4	14.	468	4
6.	220	3	15.	203	3
7.	404	4	16.	492	4
8.	467	4	17.	190	3
9.	175	3	18.	442	4
OUT	3,512	35	IN	3,705	35
			TOTAL	7,217	70

'What Pinehurst is doing here is definitely a very bold move … to take the golf course back to the original design and feel and look. Going back to rugged and natural.'
GRAEME MCDOWELL

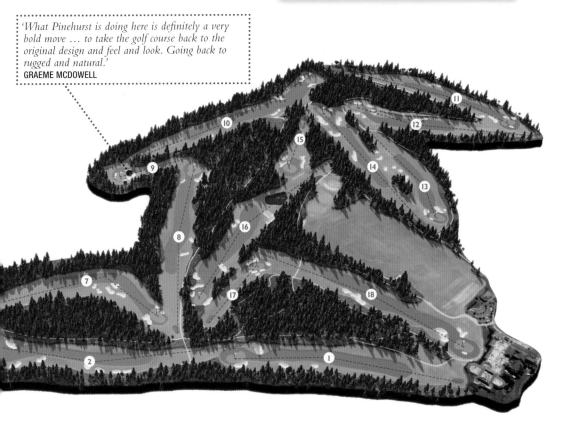

area, highlighted by Pine Needles. Unfortunately it opened in 1929, the year of the great stock market crash and the start of a deep economic depression in North America.

By the early 1960s, the concept of using golf to sell residential property led to golf courses once again being constructed, both in Pinehurst and in selected areas across the US. This time, heavy duty construction equipment was available to the architects – as opposed to the mules and drag pans with which Donald Ross worked. Yet, none of the courses built in the Pinehurst area since Ross's death in 1948 enjoys the sustained playing interest of his masterpiece, No 2.

GRADUAL EVOLUTION

Not only did Donald Ross design No 2 but he also oversaw all its significant changes and modifications. Thus it enjoyed the unheard-of luxury of having its architect lavish his personal attention on it for a 45-year period, and even to this day No 2 has a unified feel quite unlike most championship courses. The slow evolutionary process included numerous changes to its general routing. In 1908 No 2 grew to an 18-hole course, measuring under 6,100 yards, and today's 3rd and 6th holes were added in 1923. All the current holes were finally in place by 1935, when the 4th and 5th holes were created.

In that same year, thanks to advances in agronomy, Ross converted all 18 greens from sand to grass. While the course was closed, he also added 12 new back tees, partly because of the increasing switch to steel shafts for golf clubs. When it reopened in 1936, No 2 measured more than 6,950 yards and featured its now-famous greens, which were shaped like the back of a turtle and shed mis-hit approach shots off its mown sloping sides. These turtleback greens, especially at the firmness that can be achieved with modern

agronomy, provide an extremely exacting target. Though they average 5,500 square feet, more than half the technical green space does not support a hole location as such greens gradually slope off on all sides. Thus, the effective hitting area at No 2 is about 2,500 square foot, smaller than Pebble Beach's notoriously tiny greens.

PINE FOREST SURROUNDINGS

No 2 is in no way visually flashy; the only water is a small pond easily carried off the 16th tee. A game here is played on fairways through wide corridors of pine trees that culminate with sophisticated green complexes. Cumulatively as challenging as any set in the world, these greens allow Pinehurst to host the biggest events in American golf.

The course flows along with holes that give and take away. The downhill three-shot 4th, where ground can be made up, is followed by as hard a consecutive pair of holes as can be found in American golf. Indeed, Donald Ross considered the approach to the 5th as the hardest shot on the course. Regardless of the difficulty, it is almost impossible to lose a ball while playing No 2. Though the course is thoroughly testing, resort guests delight in finishing their round with the same ball with which they started.

Play concludes under the shadow of the clubhouse where members and resort guests sit in the shade on the porch, mesmerized by the vast range of recovery shots possible around the home green. Symbolic of the options around all the greens, one golfer may elect to putt up the 3-foot bank onto the green while another plays a chip-and-run into the bank. Still others pitch the ball directly onto the putting surface while some use their utility club. Therein lies the joy of No 2: these recovery shots are within the physical abilities of all golfers; whether or not the golfer has

One of the hardest shots on the course is the approach to the 5th green, angled away to the left and guarded by bunkers.

the nerve to pull off the shot is what makes the game so fascinating here.

INFINITE ATTRACTION

Golfing giants from Ben Hogan to Arnold Palmer and Jack Nicklaus to Tiger Woods have expressed their admiration for this style of golf, where short grass replaces water and thick grass as being the principal challenge. Open champion Tommy Armour summed up the allure of No 2 when he wrote: 'The man who doesn't feel emotionally stirred when he golfs at Pinehurst beneath those clear blue skies and with the pine fragrance in his nostrils is one who should be ruled out of golf for life. It's the kind of course that gets into the blood of an old trooper.'

SENSITIVE RESTORATION

In 2011 architects Bill Coore and Ben Crenshaw undertook a major restoration of No 2, removing 35 acres of invasive Bermuda rough, re-establishing the native sandy floor and disposing of 650 unnecessary sprinklers. Players once again rejoice in the fast-running conditions of the Ross era.

Harbour Town
Hilton Head Island, South Carolina

Period newspaper accounts, as well as shipping records for golf equipment from the port of Leith, in Scotland, clearly indicate that a period version of golf was being played in Charleston, South Carolina as early as the mid-1740s. The South Carolina Golf Club was chartered there in 1786 and staked its claim as America's first organized golfing club.

**The Sea Pines Resort
(Harbour Town Golf Links)**
Hilton Head Island, South Carolina

Designers: Pete Dye and Jack Nicklaus, 1969

The South Carolina Golf Club was no longer functioning by the early 19th century, but in a blindingly good public relations move the builders of Hilton Head Island's Harbour Town Links reestablished the club's charter in 1968. They moved its 'headquarters' from Charleston (some 70 miles distant) and established a small museum of ancient clubs and memorabilia. Such traditionalist trappings would surely burnish any new club's

'With Harbour Town we entered a new era in golf course architecture. It raised the bar for the rest of us. It made us all better.'
REES JONES

reputation, but this was of particular relevance at Harbour Town, because this was the layout that, quite literally, changed the face of American golf-course design.

THE DAWN OF A NEW ERA

Opened in 1969, Harbour Town was built by Pete Dye with input from Jack Nicklaus. Though not actually the first course to show Dye's innovative modern-traditionalist style (both Crooked Stick and The Golf Club preceded it), its immediate platform as permanent host of the PGA Tour's Heritage Classic gave it infinitely wider exposure. Dye, a former Ohio insurance salesman, was a fine player himself who began his design career building little-known Midwestern courses in the late 1950s. A 1963 visit to Scotland broadened his horizons, however, and soon Dye was incorporating such Old World touches as pot bunkers, blind shots and hazard-buttressing

CARD OF THE COURSE

HOLE	YARDS	PAR	HOLE	YARDS	PAR
1.	410	4	10.	444	4
2.	502	5	11.	436	4
3.	437	4	12.	430	4
4.	200	3	13.	373	4
5.	530	5	14.	192	3
6.	419	4	15.	571	5
7.	195	3	16.	395	4
8.	470	4	17.	185	3
9.	332	4	18.	452	4
OUT	3,495	36	IN	3,478	35
			TOTAL	6,973	71

2010 Heritage champion Jim Furyk playing the tee shot at the 452-yard 18th hole.

railway sleepers into his repertoire. Furthermore, with Harbour Town as an example, Dye's accent on shorter, more varied holes, smaller greens and greater strategic interest single-handedly reversed the postwar trend towards huge layouts that were heavy on challenge but light on character. Thus, with an opening day yardage of 6,655 yards (and some astonishingly high scores in the inaugural Heritage), Harbour Town provided an entirely new idea of what thoughtful course design could, and should, be about.

Though lengthened over the years, Harbour Town still opens benignly, with a pair of moderate par fours surrounding the relatively simple par-five 2nd. The initial chance to experience Dye's creative style comes at the 200-yard 4th, the first of four exciting par threes, where the left third of a typically small green is lined with railway sleepers and juts dangerously into a pond. More forgiving is the right side of the putting surface, and a safe area exists still farther right, but the challenge of going for a left-side pin is considerable.

THE SETH RAYNOR INFLUENCE

Pete Dye has long admitted to being heavily influenced by the work of course designer Seth Raynor, so it is probably not a coincidence that the 195-yard 7th – which was originally only 165 yards – bears a clear resemblance to so many Macdonald/Raynor short holes, which regularly feature greens that are almost completely surrounded by sand. At Harbour Town, their trademark horseshoe-shaped ridge built into the putting surface is absent, and several overhanging trees (which can deflect even slightly wayward approaches) differ markedly from the prototype, but the overall similarities are difficult to ignore.

The front nine then closes with back-to-back par fours of utterly varied character. The 470-yard 8th is perhaps Harbour Town's toughest hole, bending gently leftwards through a narrow, wooded driving zone, then threading through more trees to a small green guarded left by sand and water. The 9th, on the other hand, measures only 332 yards and is, theoretically at least, drivable. But its distinctive Y-shaped green has end-to-end sand in front, and several tiny pot bunkers fill the top of the Y, making it impossible to putt (and difficult to chip) from one spoke to the other.

THE UNIQUE 13TH

The back nine begins with three consecutive par fours of similar lengths but varying characters before encountering one of the club's best-known holes, the 373-yard 13th. Until this point, railway sleepers have been used to bulkhead only water hazards, but here is found a tight drive-and-pitch whose green is so buttressed, especially a narrow finger of putting surface that extends forwards into the sand. Such a design might feel faintly gimmicky today but was entirely ground-breaking in 1969 – and the concept, Dye has long

emphasized, was provided by his wife Alice, a top amateur player with a good bit of course-design knowledge in her own right.

The 192-yard 14th has grown 40 yards since its inception but still features a green guarded tightly by a pond and a nasty back-left pot bunker. The once-untouchable 571-yard 15th and 395-yard 16th (a 90-degree dogleg left where the modern waste bunker came into fashion) then lead to the windblown shores of Calibogue Sound and an extraordinary waterside finish.

AN EPIC CLOSE

First comes the 185-yard 17th, a true Dye original featuring a narrow, banana-shaped green situated on a peninsula, its left side guarded by a wide expanse of marsh and the ends of an 80-yard long bulkheaded bunker. A single, ideally placed bunker also muscles in on the right side of the putting surface, all of which combines with normally stiff breezes to make this a great one-shotter and a thrilling 71st hole of a championship.

The 18th, for its part, is a sprawling 452-yard par four, which features a peninsula of fairway extending westwards into the marshes. A tee shot successfully finding the peninsula leaves an all-carry mid-iron to a narrow, deep green situated at the water's edge. A drive, however, played safely to the right of this 90-yard wide fairway leaves a much longer approach, raising the prospect of a right-side lay-up. Both strategic and highly dramatic, it is a suitably distinctive finish for one of America's most inventive, and highly important, works of golf-course design. When asked to sum up his achievement at Harbour Town, Dye replied memorably, 'It's different, but then, so was Garbo.'

Augusta National
Augusta, Georgia

For many, Augusta National represents the epitome of the desirable golf course: an idyllic setting, a stiff challenge and an unrivalled fame that transcends the sport itself.

Augusta National Golf Club
Augusta, Georgia

Designers: Bobby Jones and Dr Alister MacKenzie, 1933
Major events: The Masters 1934–present

As perhaps *the* icon of pre-Second World War American sporting life, Bobby Jones was a unique and accomplished sportsman. In addition to claiming 13 Major championships and winning the Amateur and Open titles of both the United States and Great Britain in 1930, Jones was also an

CARD OF THE COURSE

HOLE	NAME	YARDS	PAR	HOLE	NAME	YARDS	PAR
1.	Tea Olive	455	4	10.	Camellia	495	4
2.	Pink Dogwood	575	5	11.	White Dogwood	505	4
3.	Flowering Peach	350	4	12.	Golden Bell	155	3
4.	Flowering Crab Apple	240	3	13.	Azalea	510	5
5.	Magnolia	455	4	14.	Chinese Fir	440	4
6.	Juniper	180	3	15.	Firethorn	530	5
7.	Pampas	450	4	16.	Redbud	170	3
8.	Yellow Jasmine	570	5	17.	Nandina	440	4
9.	Carolina Cherry	460	4	18.	Holly	465	4
OUT		**3,735**	**36**	**IN**		**3,710**	**36**
				TOTAL		**7,445**	**72**

'There is not a hole out there that can't be birdied if you just think; and there is not a hole out there that can't be double-bogeyed if you stop thinking.'
BOBBY JONES

educated man of the highest order. With degrees in mechanical engineering (Georgia Tech) and English literature (Harvard), he went on to study law at Emery University, passing the Georgia state bar after on three semesters and becoming, in his post-golf life, a practising attorney.

THE IMMORTAL BOBBY

Retiring from competitive play at the age of only 28, Jones decided to build a world-class golf course intended largely as a playground for him and his friends. Jones chose to locate his course not in his native Atlanta but 150 miles east in Augusta. Jones

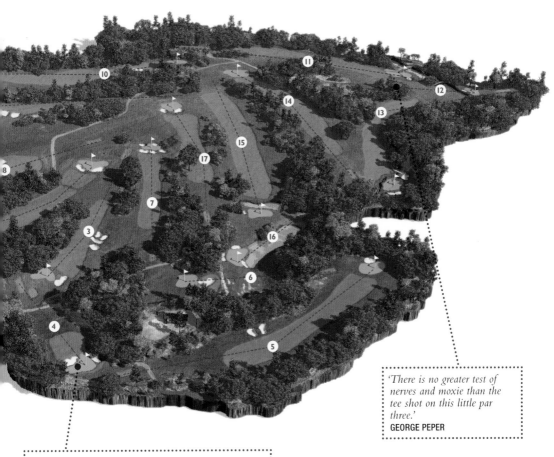

'There is no greater test of nerves and moxie than the tee shot on this little par three.'
GEORGE PEPER

Statistically, throughout the 2013 Masters, the 4th hole proved the hardest against par on the whole course.

In 2003, Scott Verplank birdied the centrepiece 12th hole at Amen Corner in all four rounds, the first player to achieve this.

selected a tract that previously housed the South's first commercial nursery, originally developed by Belgian émigré Louis Berckmans. Known as Fruitlands, the property was enviably attractive with its wide array of exotic plantings and handful of natural water hazards, but it was also surprisingly hilly, its highest point sitting nearly 150 foot above its lowest.

THE JONES/MACKENZIE PARTNERSHIP

Jones enlisted the help of the game's highest-profile architect, Dr Alister MacKenzie, to make his conceptual dream a reality. It is generally believed that MacKenzie was responsible for the course's routing, but Jones is known to have hit countless test shots during its construction, and the finished product's restrained use of sand was a marked stylistic departure from most previous MacKenzie designs. It can be reasonably assumed

that Jones's overall input widely exceeded that of most of today's player–architects.

Jones and MacKenzie shared a number of beliefs about course design. These included a primary emphasis on strategy over simple power, wider fairways to encourage the use of the driver, heavily contoured putting surfaces, the occasional green complex favouring a judicious use of the ground game and, above all, the absence of rough. Jones believed that Augusta might introduce a new sort of design to American golf – a welcoming style giving the less-skilled plenty of room to enjoy themselves while requiring the professionals to find just the right locations amid the huge fairways if they were to aggressively attack the pin on their approach. In this he and MacKenzie unquestionably succeeded, for their original design provided well-defined strategic options on virtually every shot despite incorporating a minimal 22 bunkers on opening day.

REPLICATING THE CLASSICS

While Bobby Jones stated publicly that Augusta National would not repeat any classic holes from Great Britain, Dr MacKenzie's notes indicate that their influence was, at the very least, strongly felt. On no fewer than nine of Augusta's original holes, MacKenzie drew comparisons to British models, these parallels ranging from 'embodies the most attractive features of' to being 'similar in character'.

Among the most 'similar in character' was the 6th, with its huge front-left bunker. This was MacKenzie's rendition of the Redan. Most intriguing perhaps was the 7th, today a long and penal test but in its infancy an approximation of the 18th at St Andrews (Old Course), complete with faux Valley of Sin before the putting surface. This green complex was completely remodelled in 1938, leaving no trace of the hole's noble roots.

THE MASTERS

Bobby Jones and friends inaugurated what was initially called the Augusta National Invitation Tournament in 1934, with the small, but spirited event quickly growing into The Masters by decade's end. Thus Augusta has long reigned as the only permanent site of one of golf's four Major championships, a status that has led to unmatched fame and a remarkably high degree of course alteration.

While many earlier architectural changes were made in efforts to inject more playing strategy, most of Augusta's 21st-century alterations have been triggered by the lack of meaningful regulation of modern equipment. This is a layout whose period yardages of 6,700 (1935) and 7,020 (1974) gave it a well-deserved reputation as a long hitter's haven, but which, by the new millennium, routinely witnessed Masters competitors hitting short-iron seconds into par fives such as the 13th and 15th. Logically, the course was extended to its present 7,445-yard standard. This was accompanied by the wholesale growing of rough and planting of fairway-narrowing trees – additions wholly antithetical to the design philosophies of Bobby Jones and Dr MacKenzie.

The green complexes particularly affect play on the water-free front nine, where holes such as the 2nd (with its shallow but immensely wide putting surface) and the 3rd (featuring an elevated, heavily sloped green) have their optimum lines of play vary with specific pin placements. Alternatively, the steep contouring of greens at the 5th, 6th and 7th require uncommon precision, lest a reasonably accurate approach find itself far, and several nasty breaks, from the flagstick.

The 570-yard 8th features a deep, bunkerless green surrounded by distinctive mounding, which was once removed (1956), then later restored (1979), while the 460-yard 9th is renowned for its uphill second shot to a steeply pitched putting surface – an approach that, if missed even the slightly bit short, can trickle agonizingly back a good 30 yards.

SCENE OF EPIC GOLF

No matter the quality of the outward half, it is towards Augusta's epic back nine that a golf enthusiast's attention naturally focuses, kicking off in grand style at the downhill 10th, where the tee shot, if properly turned down the left side, will run out to an impressive distance. The approach is then played across a swale to a steeply sloping putting surface that offers few easy options. Miss long or left, and five suddenly becomes a palatable score.

As the start of Augusta's famous Amen Corner, the 505-yard par-four 11th is keyed by the small left-side pond behind which much of the green is angled, a hazard so well positioned as to weaken the knees of even the world's best as they stand over the long, downhill approach.

The 12th ranks among golf's most treacherous short holes, its hourglass green angled behind Rae's Creek, with a single bunker front-centre and two more carved into the rear hillside. Two factors dominate play: the shallowness of the putting surface (particularly the far-right side) and winds that seem constantly to change in strength and direction.

TWO SUPERLATIVE EPIC PAR FIVES

Amen Corner ends with perhaps the game's greatest strategic par five, the 510-yard 13th. Playing from a new championship tee, this gem sweeps majestically leftwards, the inside of its dogleg tightly flanked by a winding tributary of Rae's Creek. Presuming a long, drawn tee ball has found the fairway, the golfer now faces a taxing decision, for the heavily contoured green may well lie within reach, but its front and right side are guarded by a particularly deep section of the creek, while back and left are menaced by a grassy swale and four large bunkers.

The 440-yard 14th is memorable primarily for its bunkerless, faintly over-the-top MacKenzie

green complex, while the15th gives the back nine its second terrific go-for-it-or-not par five. For those finding the fairway off the tee, the challenge is spine-tingling: a long, downhill second played across a pond to a shallow, steeply sloped putting surface, or a simple short-iron lay-up. But just like the 13th, laying up is no bargain, for the water may well be more unnerving on a delicate three-quarter swing than to the uninhibited rip of a long-iron – a superbly subtle gambit on Dr MacKenzie's part.

Augusta's final all-or-nothing challenge comes at the 170-yard 16th, a hole added by Robert Trent Jones in 1947 as a dramatic replacement for a much shorter original. With its huge green curving leftwards around the corner of a man-made pond, it has hosted countless memorable Masters moments, mostly on the final day when the traditional back-left pin position allows all manner of shots to funnel towards it. Pins cut on the elevated right tier – both front and back – have long proved dramatically harder, and proportionally less theatrical.

The dual par-four closers offer considerably less flair than their immediate predecessors but quite a

At this 15th hole Gene Sarazen struck 'the shot heard round the world' at the 1935 Masters: a 220-yard 4-wood across the pond.

The ever-changing face of Amen Corner
11th, 12th and 13th holes

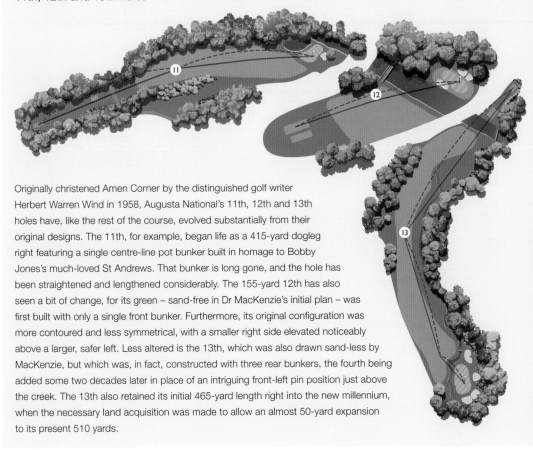

Originally christened Amen Corner by the distinguished golf writer
Herbert Warren Wind in 1958, Augusta National's 11th, 12th and 13th
holes have, like the rest of the course, evolved substantially from their
original designs. The 11th, for example, began life as a 415-yard dogleg
right featuring a single centre-line pot bunker built in homage to Bobby
Jones's much-loved St Andrews. That bunker is long gone, and the hole has
been straightened and lengthened considerably. The 155-yard 12th has also
seen a bit of change, for its green – sand-free in Dr MacKenzie's initial plan – was
first built with only a single front bunker. Furthermore, its original configuration was
more contoured and less symmetrical, with a smaller right side elevated noticeably
above a larger, safer left. Less altered is the 13th, which was also drawn sand-less by
MacKenzie, but which was, in fact, constructed with three rear bunkers, the fourth being
added some two decades later in place of an intriguing front-left pin position just above
the creek. The 13th also retained its initial 465-yard length right into the new millennium,
when the necessary land acquisition was made to allow an almost 50-yard expansion
to its present 510 yards.

measure of toughness. The 440-yard 17th, which
was originally sand-free and designed to receive a
run-up approach, today requires its drive to dodge
the famed Eisenhower tree (named for President
Dwight Eisenhower, whose tee shots regularly
challenged its air space) and a high, soft second to
carry a fronting bunker. The 465-yard 18th then
demands a long, faded drive in order to avoid a pair

of left-side fairway bunkers added in 1966, followed
by an uphill approach to a two-tiered green behind
some particularly deep sand. While perhaps not
among the world's truly great finishers, the 18th
has certainly provided its share of Masters drama –
though 72nd-hole birdies to win the Green Jacket
have been relatively few and far between, most
recently Charl Schwartzel of South Africa in 2011.

TPC at Sawgrass
Ponte Vedra Beach, Florida

Deane Beman's goal in building the TPC was to create a high-profile showpiece for the PGA Tour. In that regard he succeeded admirably, because despite being built specifically for tournament golf, the course represents a fascinating, stylish test and is surely among the very best of modern American design.

TPC at Sawgrass (Stadium course)
Ponte Vedra Beach, Florida

Designer: Pete Dye, 1981
Major events: US Amateur 1994

CARD OF THE COURSE

HOLE	YARDS	PAR	HOLE	YARDS	PAR
1.	392	4	10.	424	4
2.	532	5	11.	535	5
3.	177	3	12.	358	4
4.	384	4	13.	181	3
5.	466	4	14.	467	4
6.	393	4	15.	449	4
7.	442	4	16.	507	5
8.	219	3	17.	137	3
9.	583	5	18.	447	4
OUT	3,588	36	IN	3,505	36
			TOTAL	7,093	72

'If you fail to hit and hold this green on your second shot, you may not hit and hold it on your third.'
GEORGE PEPER

Contrary to popular belief, the fan-friendly notion of stadium golf – which includes not just large spectator mounding but also holes clustered together for more convenient accessibility and viewing – did not originate entirely with then-PGA Tour commissioner Deane Beman.

However, while Jack Nicklaus had previously incorporated such concepts into his 1976 design of long-time Canadian Open site Glen Abbey, it was Beman who, in attempting to create a marketable home course for his players and their tournament, set about perfecting them on a piece of snake-infested Florida jungle in 1981.

COMMISSION FOR PETE DYE

A famously diminutive hitter during his playing career, Beman was a fan of Pete Dye's shorter, more strategic design at Harbour Town Golf Links, a layout that, the commissioner observed, was built on a similarly featureless tract. Thus the ever-inventive Dye was hired to create the first course in what would eventually become the PGA Tour's Tournament Players' Club (TPC) network – a mixed bag of fan-oriented layouts, few of which have ever approached Sawgrass for creativity, playing interest or style.

Working off a pre-drawn plan for one of the few times in his career, Dye began by excavating huge amounts of soil with which to create the desired spectator mounding, leaving the dug-out areas to become the vast network of

At the famous and controversial island-green 17th, the golfer either hits the island or reloads – for as many tries at it takes.

water hazards that today come into play at least tangentially on nearly every hole. Ultimately, Dye's mounding grew beyond all intended proportion, yet aesthetically this intervention still somehow managed not to overshadow the golfing landscape too badly.

FAN AND PLAYER REACTION

From day one, fans took an immense liking to Sawgrass, but the initial response from Tour players was overwhelmingly negative. Most comments centred around the greens, which were

considerably contoured and fell away at odd angles. Yet amid all this criticism, Jerry Pate's winning score in the course's first Players Championship was an eight-under-par 280, with his two-stroke margin of victory coming from thrilling birdies at the 71st and 72nd holes. If that was not enough to validate Dye's fan-friendly approach, Pate's affable post-round tossing of the architect and Beman into the lake immediately adjacent to the 18th green quickly became a defining moment in the history of the PGA Tour. Still, this being the players' own course, Beman had little choice but to heed their complaints, and a range of modifications was subsequently made.

Tinkered with from time to time (including a complete greens rebuild in 2006), Sawgrass is today a layout of only modest championship length (7,093 yards), though it regularly employs several longer tees during the Players Championship, thereby extending the course to 7,215 yards.

PLAYING THE COURSE

Like many of Dye's best designs, Sawgrass begins fairly tamely, with the first real danger arising at the 384-yard 4th, where water presses flush against the angled front of a smallish, steeply sloping green. The 466-yard 5th is the first of Sawgrass's longer par fours and requires a strong tee shot to a fairway turning left to right around an enormous bunker, then a long-iron to a deep, rolling green guarded by sand and grass bunkers alike. The outward half's best two-shotter, however, may well be the 442-yard 7th, where an angled putting surface protected front-right by two huge bunkers clearly favours an approach shot played from the left, daring the golfer to drive aggressively across a 200-yard long bunker that slants up that side of the fairway.

Following the 219-yard 8th (a relatively unexciting Dye par three that can be stretched to 240 yards the front nine closes with a vintage three-shotter – the 583-yard 9th. Occasionally reachable in two by longer hitters, it is the gentlest of double-doglegs, first edging right, then back left, but each with just enough turn to materially affect tactics. A tee shot driven far down the centre of the fairway, for example, leaves the line to the green bothered by left-side trees and bunkers, whereas a drive placed close to the creek, which angles across the fairway from right-to-left, allows a more unfettered path.

Another excellent par five is the 535-yard 11th, where a long drive laid close to a large left-side bunker opens up the best angle to attack a push-up green angled left-to-right beyond sand and water. Those electing to lay up, however, must also consider these hazards, for balls placed courageously close to them are left with a fairly open pitch, while those hit safely to the left have to cope with a third shot made tricky by a small, deep bunker near the centre of the putting surface.

WORLD-FAMOUS FINISHERS

The 467-yard 14th and the 449-yard 15th are strong par fours, yet they are largely overlooked amid the excitement that surrounds the three holes immediately to follow. For as Players Championship viewers can readily attest, the real fun begins at the 507-yard 16th, a sweeping dogleg left that can surely be reached in two by every professional and most skilled amateurs – yet the slightly awkward angle of the green plus the huge danger imposed by the lake curling directly behind the putting surface add a very real dash of risk to the hole.

Then there is the 17th, which, in its quarter-century of existence, has become a genuine golfing icon, its widely photographed (and copied) island green breaking entirely new ground in the realm of all-or-nothing hazards. Annually the site of so much dramatic angst throughout the Players Championship, it is surely the most widely recognized hole – and, very likely, the most controversial – anywhere in tournament golf.

The 447-yard 18th is something of a template hole for Dye, because versions of this curving, waterside two-shotter appear on a number of his courses. This one ranks among the toughest, however, particularly considering the narrowness of the fairway, and the trees that minimize any bailout room to the right.

Seminole
Juno Beach, Florida

Seminole Golf Club is said to be the only design job the great Donald Ross ever campaigned for, and while evidence suggests that he may also have lobbied Bobby Jones a little regarding Augusta National, his infatuation with Seminole is easy to understand.

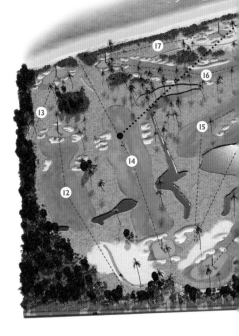

Seminole Golf Club
Juno Beach, Florida

Designer: Donald Ross, 1929

The legendary Donald Ross was perhaps the dominant player in Florida's Golden Age golf-design market, building or renovating around 40 courses statewide, nearly all of which occupied the sort of pancake-flat terrain typical of the region. Seminole, however, would be radically

CARD OF THE COURSE

HOLE	YARDS	PAR	HOLE	YARDS	PAR
1.	370	4	10.	382	4
2.	387	4	11.	420	4
3.	501	5	12.	367	4
4.	450	4	13.	168	3
5.	202	3	14.	499	5
6.	383	4	15.	495	5
7.	432	4	16.	410	4
8.	235	3	17.	175	3
9.	494	5	18.	417	4
OUT	**3,454**	**36**	**IN**	**3,333**	**36**
			TOTAL	**6,787**	**72**

different, because its site was a seaside expanse marked on both its beach and inland boundaries by a pair of high, sand-dune-covered ridges utterly incongruous to those parts. The property's mid-section was typically Florida-flat, but also ideal for the digging of drainage ponds, allowing Ross to create multiple water holes to any configuration of his choosing.

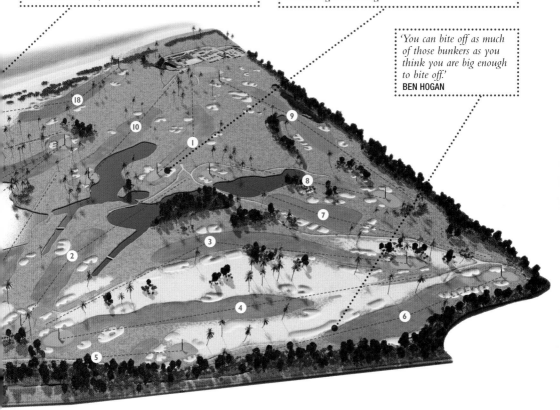

'Seminole was an exquisite job. It was heavily bunkered, 187 in all, but the bunkers were positioned and constructed to convey a sense of the nearby rolling surf.'
GEOFFREY CORNISH, 'THE ARCHITECTS OF GOLF'

Ben Hogan, practising at Seminole, complained to the club president, Christopher Dunphy, that the greens were too slow. Dunphy replied, 'If you didn't take so much time to putt the grass wouldn't get that long.'

'You can bite off as much of those bunkers as you think you are big enough to bite off.'
BEN HOGAN

A UNIQUELY SPECIAL ROUTING

But beyond simply being blessed with a superior site, there are several additional aspects of Seminole's design that set the course apart. The most obvious is a routing that manages to bring the ridges into play on 14 holes, with both nines utilizing the inland dunes and four of the final six holes filling those along the Atlantic. Also noteworthy is the bunkering, which in addition to being abundant (there are more than 175 man-made hazards quite apart from the natural stretches of sand) shows a much flashier cape-and-bay style than Ross's normally staid shaping. However, Seminole's grandest feature may simply be its ambience, because reasonably intact Golden Age courses are a rarity in South Florida, allowing the club's 1920s

The 383-yard 6th requires a left-side tee ball in order to open the optimum angle to a superbly bunkered green.

stylings – its pink stucco clubhouse, famed locker room and stately old palm trees – to shine brilliantly upon a regional golf landscape that is, for the most part, of a distinctly modern vintage.

INTO THE DUNES

Seminole begins with a pair of shortish, downwind par-fours, with the 387-yard 2nd especially standing out for its beautifully bunkered green benched into the side of the inland ridge. The 501-yard, dogleg-right 3rd features both tee and green elevated among the dunes before the challenge arrives in earnest at the 450-yard 4th, the layout's longest par four, where a right-side tee shot allows the golfer to minimize the impact of a huge bunker on the left some 40 yards in front of the green. Turning back into a three-quarter prevailing breeze, the 202-yard 5th then plays across a wide expanse of open sand to a raised green surrounded by no fewer than eight

bunkers – no simple target for long- or even mid-irons.

Play has now reached the property's inland boundary, yet despite residing far from the ocean the 383-yard 6th is surely Seminole's most celebrated hole, its photograph serving as the primary image that many hold of the club. Continuing southwards into the wind, its key feature is a line of four bunkers that begin nearly 100 yards in front of the putting surface, angling across the fairway from left-to-right all the way to the green. The ideal tee shot keeps to the left side of the fairway (close to several more bunkers) as right-side approaches face an extremely difficult angle, with the pin giving the appearance of actually being in the sand.

The 432-yard 7th (its fairway flanked by 11 bunkers, its green affected by water) and the 235-yard 8th continue this strong run before the

494-yard 9th – with a distinctly post-Donald Ross lake now flanking its right side – closes out the nine. Another pair of downwind par fours open the back nine, with the 382-yard 10th featuring the layout's sole green directly guarded by water. Often overlooked is the 367-yard 12th (whose odd, L-shaped putting surface features some tight rear pin placements), while the 168-yard 13th, its bunker-ringed green elevated against the oceanfront dunes, is comparably celebrated.

A RESOUNDING FINISH

Seminole's best run of holes comes at the finish, beginning with one of Ross's most thought-provoking par fives, the 495-yard, split-fairway 15th. Here the golfer faces a clear-cut dilemma: aim the tee ball at a small section of right-side fairway tightly squeezed between a pond and four bunkers (thus opening the ideal angle to a green now comfortably within reach) or play safely to the left, making it a three-shot hole and possibly bringing a small extension of the pond into play on the second shot.

The 410-yard 16th is similarly strategic, its right-to-left angled green challenging the aggressive player to gain a significant advantage by driving over three bunkers filling the corner of its dogleg. Then comes the 175-yard 17th, played entirely among the dunes and into a stiff, quartering breeze that makes the narrow, bunker-ringed green an extremely elusive target.

The 18th is a fine hole running parallel to the coast. At 417 yards, it is not overly long, but its elevated tee tempts the golfer to shortcut the sand-guarded dogleg, setting up the ideal angle of attack to a green hoisted among the beach-front dunes. This green, historians will note, is the design of architect Dick Wilson, who in 1947 moved Ross's original version towards the sand dunes – perhaps only one of a series of rumoured green and bunker modifications about which the club has long remained quiet.

SEASONAL ATTRACTION

Being solely a winter operation, Seminole is a seasonal bastion of affluent golfers and is thus largely reclusive. It does, however, hold a prominent amateur invitational event and, throughout the 1950s, it hosted an annual March pro-am that saw eminent golfers Lloyd Mangrum, Sam Snead, Cary Middlecoff and Arnold Palmer among its winners. The club's most impressive visitor, however, surely was Ben Hogan, who came for a month of practice each spring in preparation for the Masters. 'Seminole is the only course I could be perfectly happy playing every single day', Hogan famously concluded regarding this magnificent venue. 'If you can play well there, you can play well anywhere.'

The George L. Coleman Amateur Invitational has brought top class amateurs to Seminole since its inauguration in 1992.

Midwestern states

Despite a climate cold enough to rule out any hope of playing for at least one-third of the year, the American Midwest remains home to several states boasting long golfing histories and admirable rosters of important courses.

The most golf-mad of these states must surely be Illinois, for Midwestern golf – indeed, all American golf west of Pennsylvania – started there when Charles Blair Macdonald founded the Chicago Golf Club in 1892. By the turn of the 20th century, more than 30 additional courses had sprung up around the Chicago area, leaving it second only to New York among period American cities. And many of these layouts were of significant quality: in addition to the Chicago GC's three US Opens and four US Amateurs,

Major championship play visited the Windy City regularly before the First World War, with Glen View[1], Onwentsia[2] and Midlothian[3] all hosting US Opens, and Onwentsia adding the 1899 US Amateur as well.

A MAJOR GOLFING CENTRE

Beyond simply providing an early alternative to popular Eastern tournament venues, Chicago was also something of a second American golfing capital, with its Western Golf Association (WGA)

Medinah Country Club is home to a group of Shriners, who raise enormous sums of money for charitable work.

MINNESOTA

MICHIGAN

WISCONSIN

15 17
18

Minneapolis
St Paul

24
25
26

Whistling Straits
page 112   Sheboygan

11
12
13
14

27   Milwaukee

Oakland Hills
page 104   Detroit

Chicago
page 108   Chicago

16   Cleveland

19   Toledo

20   22
Akron

1
2
4
6
7
8
9
10

3
5

INDIANA

OHIO

Muirfield Village
page 100

21
23

28   Indianapolis
29

Columbus

ILLINOIS

Cincinnati

30

In 1938, William Langford and Ted Morrow built new holes, such as this 12th, on land adjacent to Donald Ross's course at Skokie.

taking on a major national profile, occasionally butting heads with the USGA on administrative issues and questions of amateur status. The city was also the base of operations for early course designers such as Robert and James Foulis, H.J. Tweedie and the legendary mass-producer of early links Tom Bendelow, in addition to one of the Golden Age's more overlooked design stars, William Langford. Thus by the onset of the Depression in the early 1930s well over a hundred

courses populated Chicagoland, none more prominent than five-time Major championship venue Medinah[4], whose much-altered No 3 Course remains one of the toughest parkland tests in American golf. It was the scene of Tiger Woods's first PGA Championship victory in 1999 and also of a remarkable fight-back by the Europeans to snatch victory in the 2012 Ryder Cup.

A similarly high profile is enjoyed by Olympia Fields, whose Willie Park Jnr-designed North

Course has hosted two US Opens and two PGA championships, most recently the US Open of 2003. Today Olympia Fields[5] offers 36 fine holes in suburban Illinois, but in its infancy the club was, quite literally, a town of its own, complete with the world's largest clubhouse, a private railway stop and four 18-hole courses.

Among the area's additional notables are a Donald Ross/William Langford hybrid at Skokie[6] (host of the 1922 US Open won by Gene Sarazen) and Seth Raynor's often-overlooked gem Shoreacres[7], a ravine-laden mix of original holes and Raynor's favoured replicas. Another important Ross course, sensitively restored by Ron Prichard, is to be found at the Beverly Country Club[8], venue for the 1931 US Amateur, won by Francis Ouimet, and several Western Opens, the last being in 1967, when the victor was Jack Nicklaus. It benefits from greater elevation change than most Chicago courses as it was constructed on what were once the shores of prehistoric Chicago Lake complete with dune-like sandy soil.

Chicago has enjoyed a fair amount of contemporary golf expansion, as architects Larry Packard, Ken Killian and Dick Nugent altered many older courses and added several new ones of their own, most prominently Killian and Nugent's Kemper Lakes[9], site of the 1989 PGA Championship. The area's best-known postwar layout, however, must surely be George Fazio's Butler National[10], a famously difficult course in suburban Oak Brook and, for many years, host of the Western Open.

The North Course at Olympia Fields has been much altered over the years. This is the approach to the 12th green.

The short 16th hole at The Kingsley Club is a Redan-style hole calling for a tee shot shaped in from the right.

MICHIGAN COURSES

Michigan is another state bearing a significant golfing pedigree, particularly in the Detroit area, where Donald Ross built several prominent courses and England's Charles Alison maintained a 1920s office on behalf of Harry Colt and himself. The inimitable Oakland Hills has long been the area's Major championship calling card, although clubs such as Colt and Alison's Country Club of Detroit[11], their 1921 course at Plum Hollow CC[12] in Southfield, Donald Ross's North Course at the Detroit GC[13] and Wilfrid Reid's splendidly rustic Old Course at Indianwood[14] stand out in their own right.

Michigan has also enjoyed a boom in contemporary construction on its resort-oriented Northern Peninsula, notably the links-like, daily-fee Arcadia Bluffs[15], set along the shores of Lake

Michigan, Tom Doak's Lost Dunes[16], created out of a redundant quarry, and Mike DeVries's Kingsley Club[17], in rugged country outside Traverse City, worthy challengers to the supremacy of venerable Crystal Downs[18], which ranks among America's prewar elite.

CRYSTAL DOWNS

If there is one thing that stands out about Crystal Downs, it is the golf course's utter originality. It is stocked with all manner of uniquely innovative holes, and its putting surfaces are among the most distinctive ever created by Alister MacKenzie and Perry Maxwell.

With the possible exception of his one-time partner Charles Alison, it is doubtful if any Golden Age golf-course designer travelled as much of the world as MacKenzie. He managed the impressive feat of leaving a major architectural imprint on four continents, beginning with his considerable early work in the UK, then with a whirlwind 1926 visit to Australia and New Zealand, a permanent late-1920s move to the United States and, finally, a 1930s excursion to South America. Yet even with this legacy of intercontinental wanderings, it is easy to imagine MacKenzie's reported displeasure at being diverted from a 1926 cross-country trip (from Pebble Beach to New York, en route to England) to examine a property just outside the remote northern Michigan town of Frankfort.

Travelling with his friend and partner Perry Maxwell, MacKenzie may indeed have resented this detour initially, but his mood surely changed on seeing the land in question – a rolling stretch of occasionally links-like land with commanding views of Lake Michigan and the smaller Crystal Lake. On agreeing to replace an existing nine holes of little distinction with a new 18, MacKenzie and Maxwell remained on site for several days, during which time Maxwell was once sent into town in search of supplies. Returning several hours later, he found MacKenzie seated on a hillside near the present 1st tee, boasting that he'd completed his routing of the front nine. Maxwell examined the sketch excitedly and, much to his amazement, found that perhaps the greatest golf architect of all had completed his layout with only eight holes! Clearly not wishing to alter his plans, for the 9th hole MacKenzie quickly appropriated the 175 yards of ridge on which they sat, and so it was that one of America's more distinctive par threes was created.

For many years Crystal Downs was known only to locals and a few MacKenzie cognoscenti. It is now world famous.

The front nine at Crystal Downs is essentially an open affair, played over an excitingly undulating stretch of ground with fairways framed by thick native grasses, with the really rich golf coming in the nine's latter half, beginning with the 353-yard 5th. Dog-legged to the right, the 384-yard 6th can be shortened considerably by any golfer capable of hitting over a large tree as well as an imposing bunker cluster, known as the Scabs.

The 335-yard 7th is a typical Crystal Downs hole. It requires either a laid-up iron that remains on high ground or else a drive to a lower fairway, from which the approach is at least partially blind. However, the central attraction here is the green, a huge, crescent-shaped surface whose back third is hidden from view by a broad, sand-filled hillside on the right. Similarly well regarded is the 550-yard 8th, a long dogleg right routed across the sort of rolling terrain that affords few level stances. Second shots positioned on the higher right side of the fairway leave the best angle of approach, but the hilltop green remains a tricky target from any angle. Lastly on the outward nine is MacKenzie's afterthought, the 9th, which also plays to an elevated green. This one is flanked left by a dangerous drop and has a fescue-covered hillside to the right while sand awaits an overlong shot.

Perry Maxwell oversaw construction of Crystal Downs following MacKenzie's departure for England. It is known that he took it on himself to amend Mackenzie's plans for the closing pair, though the 311-yard 17th – widely hailed as one of the game's fascinating short par fours – seems little the worse for it. Playing from an elevated tee, its 25-yard wide fairway emerges from the woods and pitches wildly to and fro before climbing to a tiny, windswept green. Potentially drivable (at least in calmer conditions), the 17th does provide a bit of room on the final uphill slope for straight attempts that come up slightly short; however,

deep greenside bunkers, plus the generally stiff breezes, still make the risk of having a go considerable.

With the heavily bunkered par-four 18th playing back across open ground, Crystal Downs completes one of golf's most attractive and varied routings. Its path incorporates spectacular scenery, strategic challenge and provides some classic MacKenzie design quirkiness to match.

NICKLAUS COUNTRY

In golfing circles, Ohio immediately brings to mind the name of favourite son Jack Nicklaus, but the game was deeply rooted in the Buckeye State long before Nicklaus ever picked up a club. Seven-time Major championship host Inverness[19] – a somewhat-altered Donald Ross classic in Toledo – is perhaps best known, although Cleveland's Canterbury[20] and Columbus's Scioto[21] (where Nicklaus learned the game) also rank highly among the region's older venues. Canterbury hosted the US Opens of 1940 and 1946, both of which had to be decided by a play-off, while Scioto's Open took place in 1926, with Bobby Jones victorious. Once held up as a bellwether of postwar design, Robert Trent Jones Snr's South Course at Akron's Firestone CC[22] has hosted three PGA championships and an endless number of PGA Tour events, though its difficult, none-too-subtle stylings no longer carry the panache they once did. However, both Nicklaus's Muirfield Village and The Golf Club[23] (Pete Dye's 1967 creation in New Albany) continue to rate among the top modern courses in the United States.

MINNESOTA AND OTHER STATES

Despite being one of America's very coldest states, Minnesota has embraced the game only since the latter years of the 19th century, with

Pete Dye's Crooked Stick ends with one of his trademark holes, curving insistently past a lake to a treacherously bunkered green.

the great majority of its top courses situated in the Minneapolis–St Paul region. A number of Golden Age designs remain central to this golfing landscape, but none more so than Interlachen[24], where Bobby Jones memorably skipped a ball across a lake at the 9th hole en route to claiming the 1930 US Open, the third leg of his legendary Impregnable Quadrilateral. Nearby Minikahda[25] also grabbed a piece of history by hosting Chick Evans's 1916 US Open victory, which formed part of Evans becoming the first man ever to claim both the Open and the US Amateur in a single season. Perhaps best known to contemporary readers, however, is a postwar course: Robert Trent Jones Snr's Hazeltine National[26], which, following blistering player criticism at the 1970 US Open, was redesigned and has since successfully hosted

another Open (1991) as well as the 2002 and 2009 PGA Championships.

While the Milwaukee CC[27] is certainly prominent (having hosted the 1969 Walker Cup), golf in Wisconsin has come to be centred around Kohler's American Club resort, which features 72 Pete Dye-designed holes, highlighted by his career-defining layout Whistling Straits. Despite more than 50 earlier courses laid out by native son William Diddell, Indiana too has seen most of its elite constructed in the modern era, led by Pete Dye's 1967 design at Crooked Stick[28] (site of John Daly's memorable triumph at the 1991 PGA), Steve Smyers's difficult-but-engaging layout at Wolf Run[29] and Tom Fazio's spectacular Victoria National[30], a water-dominated course routed through an abandoned coal mine.

Muirfield Village
Dublin, Ohio

Having modelled much of his career after that of his boyhood idol Bobby Jones, it was perhaps inevitable that Jack Nicklaus would embrace the idea of building a world-class course to host an important tournament event in his home state. It was a concept that, perhaps predictably, was hatched during a conversation with friends at the 1966 Masters.

Muirfield Village Golf Club
Dublin, Ohio

Designers: Jack Nicklaus and Desmond Muirhead, 1974
Major events: US Amateur 1992; Ryder Cup 1987; Solheim Cup 1998

It took Jack Nicklaus the better part of a decade to bring his dream course to fruition, during which time he gained invaluable architectural experience while partnering/consulting on several projects with a young Pete Dye, most notably at South Carolina's seminal Harbour Town Golf Links. Dye, in fact, prepared multiple prospective routing plans for the golf course that would eventually become Muirfield

Village, but by the time ground was actually broken Nicklaus was working with the eccentric Desmond Muirhead and Dye's early input was forgotten.

A SHARED DESIGN
Whereas Jack Nicklaus was more of a creative consultant and Pete Dye the primary designer during their time working together, it is less clear

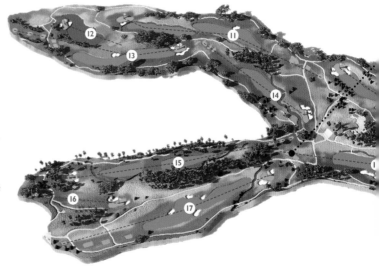

CARD OF THE COURSE

HOLE	YARDS	PAR	HOLE	YARDS	PAR
1.	470	4	10.	471	4
2.	455	4	11.	567	5
3.	401	4	12.	184	3
4.	200	3	13.	455	4
5.	527	5	14.	363	4
6.	447	4	15.	503	5
7.	563	5	16.	215	3
8.	182	3	17.	478	4
9.	412	4	18.	444	4
OUT	**3,653**	**36**	**IN**	**3,680**	**36**
			TOTAL	**7,333**	**72**

who bears the greater responsibility for Muirfield Village. Commonly held belief cites Desmond Muirhead, an experienced planner of real-estate developments, as mainly responsible for the layout's routing, with he and Nicklaus battling over each hole's design specifics thereafter. But several who were on site during the design process have said Nicklaus was overwhelmingly in charge of the entire product. In any event, their short-lived partnership dissolved soon after Muirfield Village's 1974 opening, with Muirhead going on to debase the architectural profession with 'symbolic' holes and bunkers shaped like goldfish, while Nicklaus

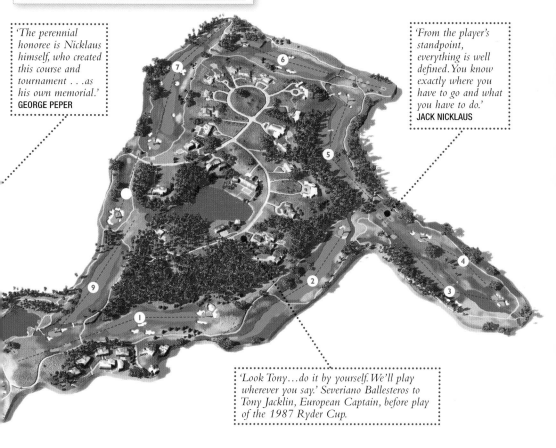

'The perennial honoree is Nicklaus himself, who created this course and tournament . . .as his own memorial.'
GEORGE PEPER

'From the player's standpoint, everything is well defined. You know exactly where you have to go and what you have to do.'
JACK NICKLAUS

'Look Tony…do it by yourself. We'll play wherever you say.' Severiano Ballesteros to Tony Jacklin, European Captain, before play of the 1987 Ryder Cup.

ventured off into one of the more prolific design careers on record.

HOME TO THE MEMORIAL TOURNAMENT

Though Muirfield Village is, in fact, the centrepiece of a real-estate development, its conception as the permanent host of the PGA Tour's annual Memorial Tournament meant that it was planned largely with professional-calibre golf in mind. Situated on a piece of rolling, frequently wooded land in suburban Columbus, it begins with the long but largely straightforward 470-yard 1st. It then grabs the golfer's full attention with a

pair of tricky par fours – the 455-yard 2nd, with a creek passing dangerously close to the right side of the green, and the 401-yard 3rd, where a tee shot played beside a left-side stream opens the best angle of approach to a shallow putting surface behind a pond.

The first hole that is truly outstanding is the 527-yard 5th, a highly strategic dogleg right. Here, the problem is the creek, which cuts in from the left side just beyond the 300-yard mark, then splits the fairway in two all the way to the putting surface. Angling leftwards beyond the water, the green clearly favours an approach played from the right fairway, a particularly difficult place to reach should the tee ball not be hit long and very straight.

MEMORABLE HOLES

The close of the front nine offers a pair of memorable holes, beginning with the 182-yard 8th, which plays across a small valley to a narrow, elevated green very nearly surrounded by two huge grass-faced bunkers. Even more dramatic, however, is the 412-yard 9th, a wooded two-shotter featuring a downhill approach to another narrow green, this one angled left-to-right behind a pond.

The inward half starts with the 471-yard 10th, a slightly uphill hole that, in 1976, was featured among the first World Atlas of Golf's best 18 holes worldwide. Curiously, though a long and difficult par four, it lacks much of the strategic flair apparent throughout Muirfield Village's best holes, two of which follow immediately in its wake.

At the 567-yard 11th hole an elevated tee encourages a long drive to a fairway flanked left by a small creek. At roughly 325 yards, the creek cuts across the fairway to guard the favoured right side of the lay-up area, before curving back in front of the heavily pitched green. A hole long enough to

Fred Couples, on the 18th hole: 'It plays very, very long with the green that slopes from back to front with bunkers everywhere.'

Nicklaus was one of the longest hitters of his day, yet a short par four, like the 14th, displays his understanding of finesse.

make even the big hitters work to get home in two, it manages to require a bit of thought on every shot – and thus it quickly became something of a template hole, reappearing in varied but similar forms on many subsequent Nicklaus designs.

Of even greater note, however, is the 184-yard 12th, an adaptation of one of Nicklaus's favourites, the illustrious one-shot 12th at Augusta National. Here Nicklaus borrowed the original's two-tiered putting surface, as well as the front-and-back bunker scheme, but then included a deeper, more elevated green and a longer carry over water.

Never was it destined to equal Alister MacKenzie's spectacular original, but as a venue for final-day tournament drama, Muirfield's version is certainly a superb alternative.

SHORTER IS BETTER?

For many years, critics of Nicklaus's work claimed that he created courses slanted heavily towards his own powerful, left-to-right style of play, yet two of

Muirfield Village's pivotal holes are of a markedly short variety. The 363-yard 14th is a gem of a two-shotter, its narrow green protected by water and sand, and greatly favouring an approach played from the creek-guarded left side of the fairway. Tumbling over hilly, wooded ground to a sharply elevated green, the 503-yard 15th is similarly engaging, being reachable in two by every player on the PGA Tour, yet routinely causing one or two key Memorial Tournament meltdowns with its creek, trees and deep greenside bunkering.

As the course's raison d'être, the Memorial has led to Nicklaus making countless changes, large and small, to the layout. But if great champions are indeed indicative of a golf course's supremacy, then Muirfield Village must surely qualify. In addition to Nicklaus himself, legendary golfers such as Tom Watson, Hale Irwin, Greg Norman and Tiger Woods have all recorded multiple wins here, while Raymond Floyd, Vijay Singh, Fred Couples and Ernie Els lead a long list of Major championship winners who have captured the Memorial title once.

Oakland Hills
Bloomfield Hills, Michigan

The more frequently a club hosts Major championships, the more regularly its fundamental design will be altered, with many of the nation's finest courses having been changed permanently just to accommodate four rounds of professional golf once every decade or so. Such has been the fate of Detroit's Oakland Hills.

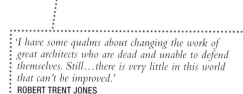

Oakland Hills Country Club (South course)
Bloomfield Hills, Michigan

Designers: Donald Ross, 1917 and Robert Trent Jones, 1950
Major events: US Open 1924, 1937, 1951, 1961, 1985, 1996; PGA Championship 1972, 1979, 2008; US Amateur 2002; US Women's Amateur 1929; US Senior Open 1981, 1991; Ryder Cup 2004

Originally built in 1917, Oakland Hills' South Course always rated among the personal favourites of its esteemed designer Donald Ross, who noted that: 'Its topographical formation could hardly be surpassed, and the area available is so extensive that I was able to lay out a very open and roomy course.' This verdict was seconded by the USGA, which quickly brought the 1924 US Open here (won by Englishman Cyril Walker) and then returned for a second national championship

'I have some qualms about changing the work of great architects who are dead and unable to defend themselves. Still…there is very little in this world that can't be improved.'
ROBERT TRENT JONES

engagement in 1937. This time Ralph Guldahl stepped to the fore, winning the title with a then-record 72-hole aggregate of 281 – guaranteeing that when the US Open returned for a third time in 1951, massive change would be in order. No matter that Guldahl was, in 1937, the finest golfer in the world, nor that the area's normally steady breezes were largely absent during his record-setting triumph. With a push from that great

The fairways look 'so narrow that you have to walk down them single file.'
CARY MIDDLECOFF

'I'm not a machine, only a golfer, and Oakland Hills was designed for some sort of super golfer that I've never seen yet. It's by far the toughest course I've ever played. And I hope I never have to play it again.'
BEN HOGAN

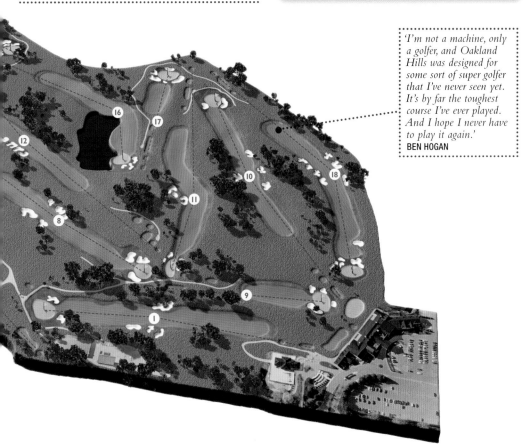

Rear view of the green at the famous 406-yard, par four 16th, with the uphill, 238-yard 17th in the background.

pioneer of USGA course modification, executive secretary Joe Dey, Robert Trent Jones Snr arrived in 1950 to set things right.

TRENT JONES'S LEGENDARY CHANGES

Performing one of the most historically significant renovations of all time, Trent Jones smartly retained all of Ross's original routing and all but one of his wonderfully contoured putting surfaces. Instead, his alterations were focused on minimizing lines of play from tee to green, removing roughly 80 obsolete bunkers and adding 66 new ones – at least 40 of which severely pinched tee-shot landing areas. Interestingly, Trent Jones added virtually no overall length to the layout; indeed, with the par-five 8th and 18th holes converted to long par fours for The Open, the 1951 layout actually played 110 yards shorter than in 1937 – but it was infinitely tougher.

The results spoke for themselves. While Ben Hogan's winning score of 287 actually matched

his previous year's winning aggregate at Merion, the reduced par of 70 placed his championship total at plus-seven, the highest relative-to-par finish since Sam Parks won with a plus-15 total of 299 at Oakmont in 1935. Providing further perspective is the fact that Hogan reached plus-seven only by closing with a remarkable 67. In his estimation, this was the finest round of competitive golf he ever played, and it prompted him to assign the course the 'Monster' nickname that it carries to this day.

Subsequently further altered by Trent Jones, Arthur Hills and, most recently, by Trent Jones's son Rees, Oakland Hills remains among the nation's most relentlessly demanding championship venues. Thanks to its Donald Ross pedigree, however, a number of really fine golf holes manage to survive within its unending rigour.

AN OVERLOOKED FRONT NINE

While the majority of the best holes are found on the back nine, the outward half does offer the

387-yard 6th, where bunkers and trees pinching the fairway suggest either an all-out drive or laid-up iron, and the 449-yard 7th, where a recently enlarged pond guards the preferred right side of the fairway and redesigned bunkers edge in from the left.

Hopefully having reached the turn relatively unscathed, the golfer begins the much-anticipated inward half with a stiff 462-yard par four before reaching one of the layout's elite holes, the 455-yard 11th. Here the ideal tee shot moves diagonally across a long stretch of rough (where both Ross and Trent Jones bunkers have been removed) to a twisting, sloping fairway guarded right by more carefully positioned sand. Once this has been safely accomplished, there remains an uphill approach shot to a narrow, saucer-like green flanked by four bunkers, rough-covered slopes to either side and a nasty slope beyond.

A BACKBREAKING FINISH

The hardest hole at Oakland Hills is very probably the 501-yard 14th, a newly enlarged par four so challenging that even Trent Jones saw no need to bunker the fairway. Apart from a relatively narrow driving area, the danger here lies mostly in the green, a large, somewhat elevated surface marked by a depression running vertically through its middle. With the resultant pin placements in its higher corners being of unusual difficulty, the 14th yielded not a single birdie during the 1951 US Open, and at its extravagant modern length it plays little easier today.

The 401-yard 15th, a sweeping dogleg left, represents the rare case of Trent Jones actually enhancing a hole's strategic possibilities. He did this by adding a bunker in the very centre of the fairway, suggesting either a laid-up tee ball or an aggressive drive squeezed between the sand and some thick left-side woods.

Oakland Hills is surely best known for the 406-yard 16th, a dogleg right played to a smallish green set attractively behind a pond. The site of a glorious Gary Player 9-iron to 4 foot that clinched the 1972 PGA Championship, this frequently photographed hole actually remains much as Donald Ross first built it. Although Robert Trent Jones Snr rebunkered the green and enhanced the dogleg by moving the fairway farther left, the fundamental challenge – whether to flirt with the water by going for the green or to search for a safe patch of short-left fairway – remains vintage Ross. Finally, the 238-yard, slightly uphill 17th and the converted par-four 18th (played as a par five by members) are notoriously difficult tournament closers.

During the 2008 PGA Championship the 7th was the third most difficult hole, playing to almost half a shot over par.

Chicago
Wheaton, Illinois

There have been many important clubs in the history of American golf, yet none has played a larger role – or had its name more prominently recalled – than that early Western outpost of the Royal & Ancient game, the Chicago Golf Club.

Chicago Golf Club
Wheaton, Illinois

Designers: Charles Blair Macdonald, 1895
and Seth Raynor, 1923
Major events: US Open 1897, 1900, 1911;
US Amateur 1897, 1905, 1909, 1912;
US Women's Amateur 1903; Walker Cup
1928, 2005; Curtis Cup 1928, 2005

Of Macdonald's original Wheaton course only the 1st, 17th and 18th holes retain their routing and hole numbers.

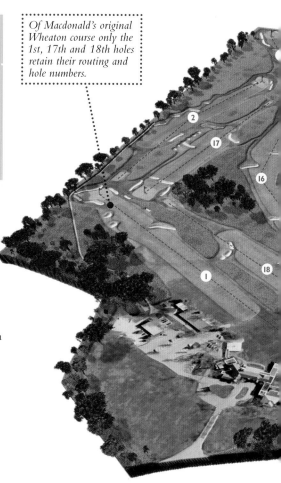

The Chicago story was written largely by Charles Blair Macdonald, who learned the game from Old Tom Morris while studying at St Andrews University in Scotland and then endeavoured to introduce it to Chicago upon his return to America in 1874. Macdonald's first recorded effort came a year later when he and a visiting St Andrews college friend batted gutta percha balls around the grounds of an abandoned Civil War-era fort. They soon gave up after, as he later wrote: 'The hoodlums in the vicinity tormented us to death.' There followed what Macdonald called the 'Dark Ages', in which he played the game only during visits back to the UK, but by 1892 he had finally gathered enough local support to build the first recorded course in the American heartland.

AMERICA'S FIRST 18-HOLER

This first Chicago Golf Club was a seven-hole affair erected on the estate of Senator C.B. Farwell, but it was soon replaced by nine holes on a suburban Belmont farm. At this point accounts differ. Macdonald himself claimed to have expanded the Belmont track to 18 holes in

During the 2005 Walker Cup an eagle two on the 5th hole by the Americans Harman and Kim set them on the way to victory.

CARD OF THE COURSE

HOLE	YARDS	PAR	HOLE	YARDS	PAR
1.	450	4	10.	139	3
2.	440	4	11.	410	4
3.	219	3	12.	414	4
4.	536	5	13.	149	3
5.	320	4	14.	351	4
6.	395	4	15.	393	4
7.	207	3	16.	525	5
8.	413	4	17.	382	4
9.	406	4	18.	425	4
OUT	**3,386**	**35**	**IN**	**3,188**	**35**
			TOTAL	**6,574**	**70**

It was 'the greatest Walker Cup that was ever played. It's the way you want to dream about going out as a captain.'
BOB LEWIS, USA WALKER CUP CAPTAIN 2005

The landscape at Wheaton is not dramatic, nor is the course long by today's standards, yet it calls for golf of a high standard.

1893, but this story is refuted by several period newspaper articles, which instead cite Chicago's third and final facility – a layout opened in Wheaton in 1895 – as the region's sole complete 18. Whatever the truth, the Chicago GC, in one location or another, enjoys the historical distinction of having possessed the first 18-hole golf course in the United States.

According to legend, Macdonald – a chronic slicer – built the Wheaton course to suit his own style of game. Though his motivation will never be known for certain, it is true that the layout all but ignored the interior of the large rectangular property. Instead, it fanned out in

a clockwise manner along the perimeter, with out-of-bounds repeatedly affecting play on the left. Such quirkiness notwithstanding, Macdonald's design quickly became one of America's elite tournament venues, hosting three US Opens and four US Amateurs between 1897 and 1912. Especially notable among these were Harry Vardon's victory in the 1900 US Open (the highlight of his ground-breaking American tour), John McDermott's triumph as the first native-born American to claim The Open in 1911, and both H.J. Whigham and H. Chandler Egan successfully defending their US Amateur Championship titles in 1897 and 1905 respectively.

ENTER SETH RAYNOR

By the early 1920s the old layout was in need of upgrading, a job for which Macdonald – now largely retired from architectural work – designated his protégé Seth Raynor. Raynor's redesign essentially represented the creation of an entirely new golf course: it maintained the corridors of play of several Macdonald holes but otherwise it reconfigured things completely. Though not significantly longer, the redesigned course was a considerably more balanced and refined test, while also introducing a number of the famous Macdonald/Raynor replica holes, none of which had been incorporated previously.

Little has changed from Raynor's day, and the present course represents one of America's grand old designs. It is laid out across mostly flat Midwestern farmland, with tall waves of native fescue and large putting surfaces defining most holes. Oak trees dot the landscape but seldom affect play, while water, in the form of a single lake, is encountered only twice. Thus in no way fancy or overbearing, Chicago is a course defined by two overriding charms. First, despite today being surrounded by suburbia, the vast expanse of the land and thickly foliaged boundaries still give the club a wonderfully isolated feel. Secondly, this course represents the quintessential demonstration of the Macdonald/Raynor design style, for its squarish greens and bunkers, and man-made contours are obviously at odds with the native terrain, yet somehow manage to feel quite natural just the same.

A FIRST-CLASS START

Chicago is not an arduous golf course, but its opening three holes can match up to almost any in the USA. It begins with a long, straightaway 450-yard par four, then turns in the prevailing wind at the 440-yard Road hole 2nd. The 219-yard Biarritz 3rd also angles into a quartering breeze, making the swale-fronted, geometrically bunkered green a particularly difficult target. With just a standard wind blowing, even the scratch golfer is pleased to reach the 4th tee at even par.

Another replica of merit is the 207-yard 7th, a longer-than-average Redan playing into the property's south-western corner. With little natural variance to the terrain, the only way to recreate the back-left fall-away and deep front-left bunker of the Redan green was to artificially elevate the entire putting surface that, like many here, is squared off at the edges. In still conditions the hole is challenging. Into the wind, it calls for a low, drawn shot of a highly skilled nature.

The closest thing to a vintage 1895 hole is the 139-yard 10th, which mirrors the forced water carry of Macdonald's old 9th, but with the trappings of the Short hole built in: two huge bunkers nearly encircling the putting surface, and not one but two horseshoe-shaped ridges. The 425-yard 18th also bears some resemblance to Macdonald's original closer, though that hole was played at 466 yards when, in the final stages of the 1897 US Open, Joe Lloyd made an improbable three to edge the soon-to-be-great Willie Anderson by one.

A NATIONAL TREASURE

The Chicago Golf Club may be done hosting US Opens, but with its shimmering native grasses, classic replica holes and a layout so unaltered that it differs by only 5 yards from that which hosted the 1928 Walker Cup, it remains among the most interesting and historic golf courses in the United States. When the Walker Cup returned in 2005 it produced a tight contest with the Americans winning by a single point, their first victory since 1997.

Whistling Straits
Sheboygan, Wisconsin

The brainchild of plumbing-fixtures magnate Herb Kohler, Whistling Straits was built as an amenity for Kohler's popular American Club resort, which already featured 36 well-known Dye holes, an inland complex known as Blackwolf Run.

The Straits course at Whistling Straits
Sheboygan, Wisconsin

Designer: Pete Dye, 1998
Major events: USPGA Championship 2004, 2010

In the 2010 USPGA the 5th proved the easiest hole with 7 eagles and 179 birdies scored during the four rounds.

For his new course at Whistling Straits, Herb Kohler wanted a waterfront layout to mirror the great links of Ireland, even though Wisconsin lies some 1,000 miles from the nearest ocean. Fortunately, however, the American Club was fairly close to the shoreline of Lake Michigan. Thus it was that one complicated land swap later, Kohler had acquired an extensive piece of lake-front property, with spectacular waterfront bluffs as high as 70 feet. Unfortunately, the property's interior, which had been a long-abandoned army training base, was essentially pancake-flat and pockmarked with roads and other military detritus, leaving a great deal of work to be done before any comparisons with Ballybunion might be even remotely in order.

A MAN-MADE MASTERPIECE

Never one to shy away from a challenge, Dye brought in enough sand to replicate the Sahara, then apportioned it entirely as he wished. The resulting metamorphosis was astonishing, even by Pete Dye's singularly innovative standard, with massive dunes springing up as needed and literally hundreds of bunkers of every shape and size being carved into the landscape. If anything, there were perhaps too many bunkers, which occasionally make strategic choices tough to delineate, but overall Dye's creation of an imaginary Irish coastline left before-and-after observers in admiring awe. In order to vary shoreline usage, Dye built each nine like a figure of eight, allowing both outgoing and returning holes to abut the lake, with the nines divided by a large, jungle-like ravine that was the property's only inland feature.

'This course is meant for length. Just look at that last hole. You've got to hit about 300 yards into the wind just to be able to get it home.'
STEVE STRICKER

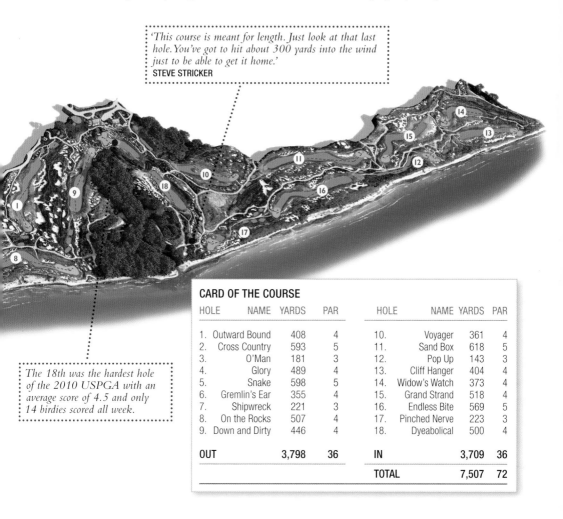

The 18th was the hardest hole of the 2010 USPGA with an average score of 4.5 and only 14 birdies scored all week.

CARD OF THE COURSE

HOLE	NAME	YARDS	PAR	HOLE	NAME	YARDS	PAR
1.	Outward Bound	408	4	10.	Voyager	361	4
2.	Cross Country	593	5	11.	Sand Box	618	5
3.	O'Man	181	3	12.	Pop Up	143	3
4.	Glory	489	4	13.	Cliff Hanger	404	4
5.	Snake	598	5	14.	Widow's Watch	373	4
6.	Gremlin's Ear	355	4	15.	Grand Strand	518	4
7.	Shipwreck	221	3	16.	Endless Bite	569	5
8.	On the Rocks	507	4	17.	Pinched Nerve	223	3
9.	Down and Dirty	446	4	18.	Dyeabolical	500	4
OUT		**3,798**	**36**	**IN**		**3,709**	**36**
				TOTAL		**7,507**	**72**

A side-view of the green at the 221-yard 7th, where there is little room to miss this putting surface in any direction.

TO THE LAKEFRONT

Following a straightforward opener and a long par-five 2nd, the first taste of the Lake Michigan shorefront comes at the 181-yard 3rd. This is a downhill, Redan-like hole where balls missed left will tumble to the beach. The 489-yard 4th is a stiff test played to a narrow bluff-top green guarded short-left by a massive, typically rough-edged bunker complex. A 598-yard affair that zigzags between lakes, the 5th is an unfortunate anomaly here, necessitated by the recreation of significant wetlands for reasons related to environmental permitting.

The drive-and-pitch 6th on the Straits Course quickly leads one back to the links-like milieu, however, before the shoreline is revisited with a vengeance on perhaps the club's most photographed hole. This is the low-lying 221-yard 7th, its deep, left-to-right angled green closer to the waves than any other Whistling Straits putting surface. There is no room to miss right here, and a large dune to the left offers comparably little bailout room. A blind tee shot away from the water begins the 507-yard 8th, followed by an approach that returns to it, the large green set into a left-to-right slope framed by a vast Lake Michigan vista.

THE INWARD HALF

The back nine starts with a pair of typically creative inland holes: the 361-yard 10th, where a single centre-line bunker some 255 yards out provides multiple tee-shot options; and the 618-yard 11th, a strategically engaging test featuring a huge bunker lined with railway sleepers and guarding the left side of the second-shot landing area. Carry this imposing hazard and a simple pitch remains; hit a seemingly easier shot to the right and a nasty front-right greenside bunker looms large.

Back along the lakefront, the 143-yard 12th is the layout's shortest hole and features one of the more interesting greens a golfer may encounter. Its left side is large and welcoming, essentially hittable with any reasonably struck ball. But this putting surface grows progressively narrower as it turns towards the water, culminating in a tiny back-right segment representing little more than a narrow spit of green wedged between dunes and a steep fall-away. With a standard lakefront breeze, this is a pin position that requires real guts to attack.

THE EPIC 17TH

Following yet another bluff-top green at the 404-yard 13th, and the temptation to shortcut the bunker-guarded dogleg at the 373-yard 14th, come some nicely varied finishing holes. The 518-yard, par-four 15th is difficult as it runs downhill towards the lake, while the 569-yard 16th is a par five that yielded no fewer than seven eagles during the 2010 USPGA. It is the 223-yard 17th, however, that truly dominates the homestretch. Its larger-than-it-looks green is angled right-to-left along a bulkheaded precipice that plunges 20 foot towards the lake. The right side of the putting surface, which is obscured by a somewhat contrived-looking bunker, does provide a bit of bailout room – but hardly enough for comfort.

The 500-yard, two-shot 18th is a quirky and demanding driving hole, and not to every golfer's taste. Its 18,000-square-foot, shamrock-shaped putting surface feels manifestly over-the-top and is rather at odds with the less-flashy nature of the other 17 greens. It proved the hardest hole against par in the 2010 PGA.

TRULY A WORLD-CLASS TEST

Whistling Straits successfully hosted Vijay Singh's play-off victory in the 2004 USPGA and Brad Bryant's triumph at the 2007 US Senior Open. Singh's winning total of 280 was the PGA's highest in 14 years and was recorded in only a modest breeze, suggesting that in a strong wind the Straits Course – despite its highly strategic underpinnings – must certainly rank among the very hardest on Earth. In 2010 a play-off was needed to separate Martin Kaymer and Bubba Watson who had tied on scores of 277 (-11). The 10th, 17th and 18th were used to determine the PGA champion, Kaymer triumphing by one shot.

The 17th was the hardest short hole of the 2010 USPGA and the fourth most difficult on the entire course.

Central states

With a four-hole course reportedly being played on a Burlington, Iowa farm during the summer of 1883, and Scottish émigré Alex Findlay batting a ball about the Nebraska prairie in 1887, golf laid some very early roots in America's central states.

Much of this region's vast, wide-open countryside is topographically limited, and its central and southern sections regularly bake under scorching summer heat, making the great majority of early courses basic affairs faced with considerable agronomic hurdles. Consequently, this is probably the only region of the United States where contemporary courses, as a whole, consistently outshine their Golden Age brethren – frequently by a wide margin.

A conspicuous exception lies in Kansas where Prairie Dunes, Perry Maxwell's seminal

The 185-yard 7th hole at Castle Pines is the shortest hole on this Jack Nicklaus course in Colorado's Front Range.

MONTANA

28

25

27

Helena

IDAHO

Boise

WYOMING

NORTH DAKOTA

SOUTH DAKOTA

26
Pierre

9
Sand Hills
page 126

8

10

NEBRASKA

Lincoln

IOWA

11 Denver
12
Colorado
Springs

COLORADO

Prairie Dunes
page 122

KANSAS

1
3
Topeka

Kansas City

4
6
7
St Louis

Jefferson
City

2

MISSOURI

5

Santa Fe

22
24

23

NEW MEXICO

14 13
15 16
Oklahoma City

OKLAHOMA

18
19
17 21

TEXAS

Austin

20

links-style layout, remains one of America's uniquely attractive courses more than 70 years after the opening of its initial nine holes. Most of the state's other top courses are found in the Kansas City area, led by the venerable Kansas City Country Club[1] – an A.W. Tillinghast design that launched Tom Watson on the road to fame – and a pair of far newer tests, Tom Fazio's Flint Hills National[2] and Tom Weiskopf and Jay Morrish's Shadow Glen[3]. Sadly, these are private. Public courses have not yet equaled their level.

MAINLY MODERN COURSES

In Missouri, the St Louis area was an early centre of play, but only one of its Golden Age courses can truly rank among the region's elite; it is Charles Blair Macdonald and Seth Raynor's St Louis Country Club[4], site of the 1947 US Open and the 1921 and 1960 US Amateurs. On the modern side, Gary Nicklaus's Dalhousie GC[5] (located in Cape Giradeau) is often rated the state's best and features a bit more rustic appearance than most entries in the Nicklaus family portfolio. A pair of

Tom Doak has rewarded the O'Neal brothers with a golf course that takes advantage of the ground contours.

Jack Nicklaus embraced the huge potential of the Nebraska sandhills with his benchmark course at Dismal River.

Robert Trent Jones Snr standards – Old Warson[6] and three-time Major championship site Bellerive[7] – also deserve a mention, though being built in 1955 and 1960 respectively these layouts can now be chronologically linked far more closely with the Golden Age than the modern.

DUNES AND BIGGER HILLS

Seldom viewed as a golfing centre during the century that followed Alex Findlay's early adventures, Nebraska has become an object of much attention since the arrival of Bill Coore and Ben Crenshaw's spectacular Sand Hills in 1995. Perhaps the finest American course built since the Second World War, its dunes-covered landscape

was bound to draw imitators to the state's west–central region, an assemblage led by the public Wild Horse[8] in Gothenburg and, more recently, Jack Nicklaus's stunning design at Dismal River[9]. Geographic inaccessibility and a sparse population are likely to limit large-scale development in this region, yet the links-like nature of the rolling, treeless terrain will surely draw further entries before the financial cup runs dry.

One such example lies in nearby north-eastern Colorado, where comparable terrain allowed Tom Doak to fashion a similarly authentic test at Ballyneal[10], just outside the farming town of Holyoke. However, most Colorado courses of distinction lie in more developed areas, and

A view of the 20th hole at Paa-Ko Ridge, a beautiful and
challenging 27-hole public course designed by Ken Dye.

virtually all of the best older designs are around Denver, where recently restored, six-time Major championship venue Cherry Hills[11] has perennially garnered most of the acclaim. Modern development was for many years centred along the north–south axis of Interstate 25, particularly on the southward run to Colorado Springs, where Jack Nicklaus's design at Castle Pines[12] served as long-time host of the now-defunct International Tournament on the PGA Tour. In recent years, however, new courses have been springing up regularly within the enormously scenic valleys that dot the Rocky Mountains, as the region continues to transform from skier's paradise to a year-round recreational destination.

Despite its stifling summer heat, Oklahoma embraced the game fairly early, helped by the presence of Perry Maxwell who, in addition to partnering with Alister MacKenzie for a spell, lived and built some 18 courses there. Most notable among these is the state's consensus number one layout – seven-time Major championship host Southern Hills[13] – but here again many more of the best are of a modern vintage. Pete Dye's Oak Tree[14] (site of the 1984 US Amateur and 1988 PGA) carries the highest national profile among these newer courses, but Tom Fazio's designs at Oklahoma State University's Karsten Creek[15] and the Golf Club of Oklahoma[16] generally draw comparable acclaim.

NURSERY TO MANY FAMOUS GOLFERS

Few states offer more golfing history than Texas, which groomed Hall-of-Famers Ben Hogan, Byron Nelson, Jimmy Demaret, Lloyd Mangrum and Ralph Guldahl within a single era, and players such as Jack Burke Jnr, Lee Trevino, Ben Crenshaw and Tom Kite thereafter. Curiously,

though, the state has produced precious few nationally prominent courses, particularly prior to the Second World War when difficult agronomic conditions helped limit the elite to 1941 US Open site (and perennial PGA Tour stop) Colonial[17] and nearby Brook Hollow[18], an A.W. Tillinghast design restored by Bill Coore and Ben Crenshaw in 1992. In the modern era, once-prominent tournament venues such as Dallas's Preston Trail[19] and San Antonio's Pecan Valley[20] (site of the 1968 PGA Championship) have been pushed aside by a spate of newcomers, with more than 800 courses now in play state-wide. Yet despite so much new course construction, only Tom Fazio's Dallas National[21], a 2000 design situated south-west of downtown Dallas, draws serious attention for consideration among the nation's best.

The region's remaining five states – New Mexico, Idaho, Montana and the Dakotas – are spread across many miles and, for the most part, feature virtually no classic courses of prominence. But, with the growth in modern holiday / retirement homes there, some striking newcomers have appeared. In New Mexico, Jack Nicklaus's 36 holes at Las Campanas[22] is particularly noteworthy, as are Ken Dye's Paa-Ko Ridge[23] and Baxter Spann's Black Mesa[24], while Idaho is led by Jim Engh's slightly over-the-top Club at Black Rock[25]. Sutton Bay[26] – a dune-filled Graham Marsh design in Agar, South Dakota – represents the consensus choice as the Dakotas' best, but it is Montana, an increasingly popular holiday and second-home destination, that has begun producing the most noteworthy courses. Tom Fazio's Stock Farm[27] and Iron Horse[28] set the present state-wide standard, but this high-growth market promises to attract an increasing number of worthy challengers in the years immediately ahead.

Prairie Dunes
Hutchinson, Kansas

Prairie Dunes Country Club in Kansas lies almost precisely at the centre of the continental United States, far distant from major oceans. Yet ironically the rolling, dunes-covered terrain to the north-east of Hutchinson are most probably the closest approximation of the game's most hallowed seaside terrain in North America.

'Coore and Crenshaw, in renovation, worked closely with the club to devise a plan to dramatically increase the amount of short grass around the greens. Once completed, all golfers, no matter what their skill level, delighted in the additional short game recovery options.'
RAN MORRISSETT

Prairie Dunes Country Club
Hutchinson, Kansas

Designers: Perry Maxwell, 1937 and
J. Press Maxwell, 1957
Major events: US Women's Open 2002;
US Women's Amateur 1964, 1980, 1991;
US Senior Open 2006; Curtis Cup 1986

CARD OF THE COURSE

HOLE	NAME	YARDS	PAR	HOLE	NAME	YARDS	PAR
1.	Carey Lane	432	4	10.	Yucca	185	3
2.	Willow	161	3	11	Honey Locust	452	4
3.	Wild Plum	355	4	12.	Briar Patch	390	4
4.	Hilltop	168	3	13.	Sumac	395	4
5.	Quail Ridge	438	4	14.	Cottonwood	370	4
6.	Cedar	387	4	15.	The Chute	200	3
7.	Southwind	512	5	16.	Blue Stem	415	4
8.	The Dunes	430	4	17.	Pheasant Hollow	500	5
9.	Meadowlark	426	4	18.	Evening Shadows	382	4
OUT		**3,309**	**35**	**IN**		**3,289**	**35**
				TOTAL		**6,598**	**70**

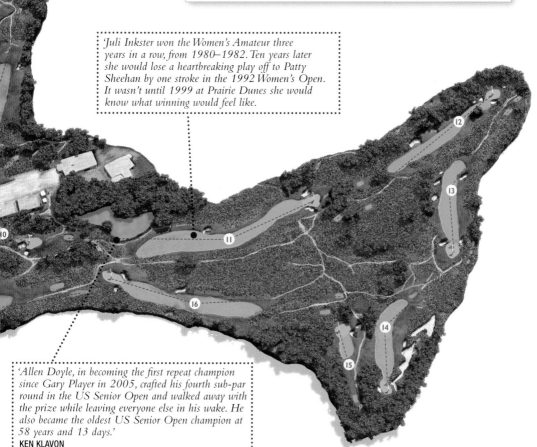

'Juli Inkster won the Women's Amateur three years in a row, from 1980–1982. Ten years later she would lose a heartbreaking play off to Patty Sheehan by one stroke in the 1992 Women's Open. It wasn't until 1999 at Prairie Dunes she would know what winning would feel like.'

'Allen Doyle, in becoming the first repeat champion since Gary Player in 2005, crafted his fourth sub-par round in the US Senior Open and walked away with the prize while leaving everyone else in his wake. He also became the oldest US Senior Open champion at 58 years and 13 days.'
KEN KLAVON

Unlike the more recently developed Sand Hills region of Nebraska, nobody had to travel great distances to discover the site on which the Prairie Dunes Country Club sits. The club was built by the Carey family, a local salt-mining clan whose love of golf led them to develop a remarkable five courses in this landlocked town with a 1930s population of 25,000. Of this quintet Prairie Dunes is easily the best, due not only to its superior terrain but also to the Careys' selection of Perry Maxwell as their architect.

FATHER THEN SON

Perry Maxwell, a Kentucky native turned Oklahoma banker, was a man of means, building his first course (Dornick Hills) on his own land in Ardmore before later partnering Dr Alister MacKenzie for three years, handling construction on several of MacKenzie's prominent American projects. Widely remembered for the scale and contouring of his putting surfaces, Perry Maxwell took full advantage of the rare opportunity that was Prairie Dunes, producing a course whose genuinely British style was extremely unusual in prewar American golf. The layout in play today is, however, only half Perry Maxwell's work – the economic realities of the Depression limited its initial construction to nine holes. It was Perry's son J. Press Maxwell who in 1957 seamlessly blended nine entirely new holes to his father's original nine.

To play Prairie Dunes is to encounter a particularly skilful blend of the natural and the man-made. The natural is represented in the

At only 355 yards the 3rd hole is not physically demanding, but the tee shot is played diagonally over dense plum thicket.

setting for beyond the sandy, dunes-covered landscape the property is bathed in a sea of tall native grasses, plum thicket, yucca plants and, in its north-east reaches, a decidedly unlinks-like, but thoroughly charming, grove of cottonwood trees. The man-made, on the other hand, comes in the form of the Maxwells' skilled, highly authentic contouring, not just on the ever-undulating greens but also across the fairways, where a good deal of hand-shaped pitch-and-roll results in very few level lies. Throw in one final natural feature, the constant Kansas winds, and Prairie Dunes is a healthy challenge for any golfer.

THE FAMOUS 2ND

After a long but fairly nondescript opener, the golfer faces a sterner test at the 161-yard 2nd, a visually striking, slightly uphill par three. The problems here are many: the green, which angles towards ten o'clock, is particularly ill-suited to the prevailing left-to-right cross-wind. Further, it is backed by a large, thicket-covered dune and otherwise surrounded by five bunkers, the largest, which sits front and centre, being some 10 foot deep. A back-left pin is particularly difficult, but three is a solid score no matter where the hole is cut.

Following the 168-yard 4th played to a similarly elevated green, three of Press Maxwell's 1957 additions – all solid, none overwhelming – set the scene for the challenge that is the club's most recognized hole, the 430-yard 8th.

ONE OF AMERICA'S BEST

Selected by *Sports Illustrated* as one of America's 18 best in 1966, the 8th is a long dogleg right favouring a drive carved into the prevailing left-to-right cross-wind – the green being completely visible only from the left side of the heavily contoured fairway. The approach is then slightly uphill to one of Prairie Dunes's most undulating greens, which is guarded front-right by a cluster of tiny bunkers.

Widely considered to be of comparable merit is the 426-yard 9th, yet it is the 185-yard 10th that is recorded as Perry Maxwell's personal favourite. Like the 2nd (and, for that matter, all of Prairie Dunes's par threes), it plays slightly uphill, this time to a small, tabletop green guarded front-right by a notably deep bunker. Wind is once again a huge factor, for it is generally directly at a player's back, making the holding of the elevated, exposed green a significant challenge.

The 452-yard 11th features a classic strategic test: whether to drive close to a left-side fairway bunker and thicket or to face a long approach to a shallow green angled behind sand and in front of a prominent mound that deflects most run-up shots.

COTTONWOODS AND NATIVE GRASSES

Then comes a stretch of four holes in which the cottonwoods can affect play, most obviously at the 390-yard 12th, where the approach must avoid several of the tallest trees, and the 370-yard 14th, whose green is recessed within an ancient grove. Although hardly typical of true links golf, the trees do provide welcome shade from the intense summer sun, which is of more importance in Hutchinson than at St Andrews.

The modern player may feel the need to reach the straight 500-yard 17th in two, but finding this green – a tiny, elevated, hump-backed affair – is especially difficult with the prevailing wind blowing against a large yucca-dotted bunker left and a steep bank right. Though only 382 yards long, the 18th is similarly appealing, drifting between walls of native grass to an angled, heavily bunkered green. Little altered by contemporary hands, Prairie Dunes remains a timeless classic.

Sand Hills
Mullen, Nebraska

When it opened for play in June 1995 Sand Hills Golf Club was appreciated for being one of the most natural courses built in the United States since the First World War.

Sand Hills Golf Club
Mullen, Nebraska

Designers: Bill Coore & Ben Crenshaw, 1995

'The greatest hazards are "alive," just sitting there saying, "Here I am – I have always been here and you need to deal with me."'
BILL COORE

Given the origins of the game along the North Sea, golf has always enjoyed an element of escapism, a sense of getting away from it all. In an ever-crowded world, this sensation becomes more cherished. Fortunately, ease in modern travel allows golfers access to out-of-the-way places. As a result, golf clubs and resorts from the Oregon coastline in the United States to Bali to Tasmania in Australia have been developed in recent times which before would not have been economically viable. One such club is Sand Hills Golf Club, located in the expansive sand-hills range in north central Nebraska.

'It's discovery, not creation. All we do is scrape off the existing vegetation and seed.'
BEN CRENSHAW

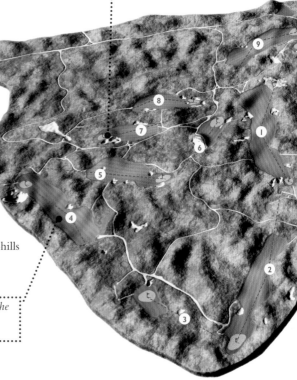

CARD OF THE COURSE

HOLE	YARDS	PAR	HOLE	YARDS	PAR
1.	549	5	10.	472	4
2.	458	4	11.	408	4
3.	216	3	12.	417	4
4.	485	4	13.	216	3
5.	412	4	14.	508	5
6.	198	3	15.	469	4
7.	283	4	16.	612	5
8.	367	4	17.	150	3
9.	402	4	18.	467	4
OUT	**3,370**	**35**	**IN**	**3,719**	**36**
			TOTAL	**7,089**	**71**

Youngscap noted: 'Not all sand hills are created equally.' An option on 8,000 acres was secured in August 1990, and Ben Crenshaw and Bill Coore made their first visit to the site the following month.

Numerous visits followed over the next two years and by spring 1993 Crenshaw and Coore had discovered more than 130 holes, from which 18 were selected and a routing plan finalized. During that year, most of the work on the site was concentrated on the irrigation system, which comprised 85 per cent of the total golf-course construction cost. Fairways, greens and tees were created by mowing existing vegetation to ground

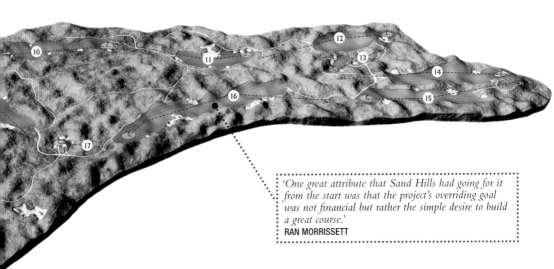

> 'One great attribute that Sand Hills had going for it from the start was that the project's overriding goal was not financial but rather the simple desire to build a great course.'
> **RAN MORRISSETT**

SUPERB TERRAIN FOR GOLF

The credit for finding and providing this primal reunion of golfer with nature belongs to Dick Youngscap and his partners. Long aware of the great sand-hills range and of the Ogallala aquifer, Youngscap searched this unique area for several years looking for property with landforms that might yield holes of high golfing quality. As

level, then tilling all areas to a depth of 6 inches. After minor grading to finish on the greens, all that was needed was to apply seed, fertilizer and water.

Such a straightforward process highlights how little of the land was disturbed during the construction of the course. Furthermore, due to the excellent sand particles, the cost per Sand Hills green was less than one per cent of that of

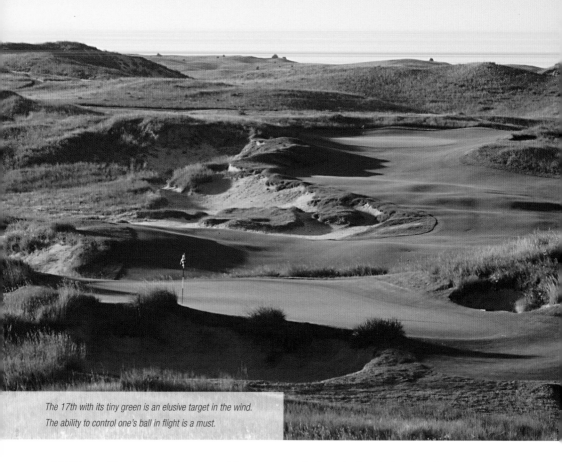

The 17th with its tiny green is an elusive target in the wind. The ability to control one's ball in flight is a must.

USING THE NATURAL ELEMENTS

a USGA specification green because neither drain tile/gravel under the greens nor special greens mix was required.

Consistent with the huge scale of the place, the course enjoys massive fairways 50–90 yards wide, which weave in and out and over and around the sand hills in every possible manner. This is a consequence of Bill Coore and Ben Crenshaw's marvellous routing, where they were more interested in following nature's lead and in finding the best holes than they were in having a formulaically balanced course of five par fours, two par threes and two par fives per nine holes. Thus, the final sequencing of the holes that they settled on was certainly not conventional. The 1st is a three-shotter, and there is not another par five until the 14th. The 7th and 8th are short two-shotters but, as they lie in opposite directions, they rarely play the same in the windy environment.

Nonetheless, the challenge to route 18 consecutive holes that played well together in all wind conditions was a monumental one. Shaped by the elements over thousands of years, the unique natural landforms were of great beauty and all parties concerned agreed that as many of them as possible needed to be included in the final course. In addition, the game of golf is a walking one, and the green-to-tee walks needed to be short. Patience was required to find such a layout, and Bill Coore and Ben Crenshaw walked the property for 30 months before settling on the routing that yielded the best 18-hole sequence.

Another crucial task was the detail work on and around the greens, which is the heart and soul of any course. Here, Coore and Crenshaw reintroduced the all-important (and all-but-dead) art form of tying the entrances of the greens to the greens themselves. The majority of the greens are open in front, allowing the course to play well in all winds.

A LINKS COURSE FAR FROM THE SEA

In all respects other than its physical proximity to water, Sand Hills plays like a links course. And, like the great links in the United Kingdom, the wind comes from all directions and so to discuss the holes at Sand Hills in terms of par is meaningless. One day, a 3-wood reaches the 283-yard 7th, while the next day the golfers need to punch a 7-iron low and under the wind for the second shot. The 16th hole at more than 600 yards can be reached in two downwind or requires a wood for the third shot if played into the wind. Typical inland courses do not possess this day-to-day variety.

Also, like the great links, a walk around Sand Hills is a study in hazards, both in bunker placement and bunker construction. Coore's favourite quote on bunkers comes from Robert Hunter who wrote in *The Links* that bunkers 'should have the appearance of being made with carelessness and abandon with which a brook tears down the banks which confine it, or the

wind tosses about the sand of the dunes…forming depressions or elevations broken into irregular lines. Here the bank overhangs, where there it has crumbled away.' Coore must have been pleased by his design team's handiwork as that is exactly the effect that they achieved at Sand Hills. Indeed, as man's hand feels very light in the construction of the entire course, all golfers feel a strong reconnection with nature when playing here.

INTRIGUING GOLF HOLES

For all the sensitivity displayed towards nature throughout the construction process, the quality of the individual golf holes remains what matters most. After all, in order for its members (there are only 160 of them) to want to travel great distances to get here, the prospect of playing the holes must be an enticing one. Starting with the false front at the 1st green, which can send balls 20 yards back off the elevated green, the course is rich with vexing features. How best to use the slope left of the 3rd green to feed the tee ball onto the large green is a shot that a golfer never tires of playing.

Though plenty of big hitting is required across the rolling topography, as highlighted by the 472-yard 10th and 467-yard 18th, the holes that require the most finesse are often cited as among the game's finest. Examples include the eminently drivable 283-yard 7th, the 508-yard 14th with its small green angled against a dune and the one-shot 150-yard 17th. This wide variety of challenge makes the course such a delight to play, year after year.

Coore, characteristically modest, stated: 'The Sand Hills site was ideal. The challenge there was to create a course equal to the potential of the land. To have constructed anything less than an extraordinary golf course on that site would have been a failure.'

West coast states

According to rumour, the game of golf first appeared in Riverside, California in 1891, and on Catalina Island and at several sites in the northern half of the state a year later. As a matter of generally accepted fact, it began in both the San Francisco Bay area town of Burlingame and in Riverside in 1893.

In the Bay area, golf caught on quickly, with several more documented facilities in existence prior to the dawn of the 20th century, and a fine list additions opening during the Golden Age. The Olympic Club's Lake Course remains one of the perennial landmarks, while less celebrated layouts include Dr Alister MacKenzie's Meadow Club[1], Willie Watson's Orinda CC[2], which features holes named Inspiration, Despair and Gibraltar, and George Thomas and Billy Bell's now-altered layout at Stanford University[3] on which both Tom Watson and Tiger Woods played college golf.

Flamboyant bunkers were a feature of many of MacKenzie's later courses, such as on the short 18th hole at Pasatiempo.

WASHINGTON

Portland

OREGON

32 ⚑ Pacific Dunes
33   *page 142*

NEVADA

UTAH

⚑ 31

1 ⚑
Olympic Club   San Francisco
page 148   ⚑ 2
7 ⚑   3
   4
Pebble Beach   5
page 152   ⚑ 6
8 ⚑

Cypress Point
page 158

CALIFORNIA

Spyglass Hill
page 162

30 ⚑ Mesquite

Las Vegas ⚑ Shadow Creek
28   *page 138*
29

ARIZONA

9 ⚑   12
   ⚑ 13

Riviera   21 ⚑ Flagstaff
page 166   23

Los Angeles ⚑ 10   Palm Springs   22 ⚑
   11   ⚑ 17   24 ⚑
14 ⚑   18   25   Scottsdale
15 ⚑ San   19   26 ⚑ Phoenix
16   Diego   20   27

Kauai
39 ⚑   *Oahu*
40   Honolulu ⚑ 34   *Maui*
   35   ⚑ 38
HAWAII   *Hawaii*
   36 ⚑
   37

The Pacific Ocean beckons beyond the 10th green on the Dunes Course of the Monterey Peninsula Country Club.

SAN FRANCISCO GOLF CLUB

No account of the finest golf courses in and around San Francisco would be complete without mention of the San Francisco Golf Club[4], one of the oldest clubs in the west, having been founded in 1895. It began within the confines of the former Presidio military base, adjacent to the Golden Gate Bridge, the club moving twice before settling into its present site along the city's southern boundary, just south-east of Lake Merced. This was an area destined to become a competitive golfing centre: by the mid-1920s The Olympic Club had built 36 holes just across the lake; Harding Park's[5] fine municipal 18 occupied the northern shore; and the Lake Merced Country Club[6] was completed less than half a mile to the

south. This gave San Francisco a cluster of first-class courses — and professional championship venues — to be envied by almost any city in America.

Within this closely situated group, only the San Francisco Golf Club has elected not to embrace major tournament play, the sum total of its national events being a single PGA Match Play title in 1938 and the 1974 Curtis Cup. Such assiduous avoidance of the spotlight has allowed the club to maintain a degree of reclusive anonymity almost unsurpassed in American golf. This in turn has made its splendid course one of the least seen among the nation's elite.

Strangely, the architectural history of the present San Francisco layout has long been a puzzle. Its creation has been officially attributed to A.W. Tillinghast – that stalwart of eastern Golden Age design – though in reality his 1920 work represented alterations to a course already in place, and of unknown origin. Tillinghast was not particularly well established in the late 1910s and, so far as is recorded, had never ventured west of San Antonio before being hired.

Making matters more curious is San Francisco's trademark bunkering, which is of a scale and style visibly at odds with almost all of the Tillinghast portfolio. Where Tillinghast focussed mostly on intimidating greenside hazards, San Francisco features scores of fairway bunkers placed at varied angles and distances, and their considerable scale and flowery shaping is in stark contrast to his more restrained norm.

Like many Golden Age courses, this once wide-open, wind-exposed layout is today largely tree lined, ranking San Francisco's rolling, cypress-bordered fairways among the most attractive in American golf. Charm lies in the fact that 15 of its 18 holes are un-altered strategically since before the war. In 2005, Tom Doak was hired to restore, as faithfully as possible, the three Tillinghast originals.

FURTHER CALIFORNIAN ABUNDANCE

Moving down the coast from San Francisco, in Santa Cruz lies MacKenzie's Pasatiempo[7] (where he lived in a house by the 6th fairway for his final years) while on the Monterey Peninsula Pebble Beach and Cypress Point have remained household names to golfers everywhere. The Bay area lacked land for widespread postwar course development, but Monterey's golfing growth has continued well into the modern era, with Spyglass Hill opening in 1966 and the Links at Spanish Bay[8] (Robert Trent Jones Jnr, Sandy Tatum and Tom Watson) following in 1987.

In southern California, Santa Barbara features another MacKenzie gem, the Valley Club of Montecito[9], while the state's southernmost regions – Los Angeles, San Diego and Palm Springs – each boast extensive golfing histories. In Los Angeles, where nearly as many fine courses have been lost as still exist, George Thomas's famous 'triumvirate' excel: Riviera, the North Course at the Los Angeles CC[10] and his uniquely routed canyon course Bel-Air[11]. Sherwood[12] – a Jack Nicklaus

George Thomas's course at Bel-Air Country Club has been a second home for Hollywood stars since it opened in 1925.

The 206-yard 6th on the North Course at Torrey Pines may play 40 yards shorter when the wind is in the golfer's favour.

design in suburban Thousand Oaks – is notoriously upmarket, while Moorpark's Rustic Canyon[13] (Gil Hanse and Geoff Shackelford) is one of the west coast's most thought-provoking public courses. San Diego has long been known for Dick Wilson's 1960s design at La Costa[14], as well as for 36 public holes at scenic and exceptionally tough Torrey Pines[15], host to the 2008 US Open. Max Behr's Rancho Santa Fe CC[16] (1929) and several nearby newcomers cannot be overlooked.

And there is Palm Springs, which is virtually a golfing university of its own with well over a hundred courses laid out across the Coachella Valley's vast desert floor. Unfortunately, the general sameness of terrain has led to a rather uniform standard of design, with distinctly man-made water hazards frequently providing the lion's share of the test. Thankfully, most of the area's best courses also rank among its least stereotypical, with Pete Dye's Mountain Course[17] at La Quinta utilizing higher terrain, Tom Doak's Stone Eagle[18] taking this concept to greater heights and Tom Fazio's Quarry at La Quinta[19] offering all manner of interesting (if entirely man-made) features. Pete Dye's Stadium Course at PGA West[20] ranks among the hardest courses ever built.

MODERN DESERT COURSES

Few states have seen greater modern golf development than Arizona, much of it taking place around Scottsdale and in more temperate getaways (for example, Flagstaff and Prescott) to the north. Arizona is also responsible for spawning the modern concept of American desert golf: a forced-carry, target-oriented game necessitated by water-conscious state laws limiting new courses to a maximum of 90 acres of maintained turf. The result, once again, is a certain sameness of style, yet northern layouts such as Pine Canyon[21], The Rim[22] and both the Canyon and Meadow courses at Forest Highlands[23] provide welcome variety. Like Palm Springs, Scottsdale's best courses often gain their edge by utilizing attractive mountain terrain, most notably Tom Fazio's Estancia Club[24], Jack Nicklaus's Desert Highlands[25] and his six-course mega-complex at Desert Mountains[26]. On the older side, Carefree's Desert Forest[27], an ultra-natural 1962 Red Lawrence design, is a favourite throughout the region.

The last of the West's desert states, Nevada, was a true latecomer to the game, with nearly all of its top courses being modern tests in the vicinity of Las Vegas. Casino mogul Steve Wynn's Shadow Creek is by far the state's highest-rated course, with Rees Jones's Cascata[28] and the Nicklaus-designed complex at Lake Las Vegas[29]

There are no fewer than six courses in the stable at PGA West.

The 363-yard 7th at Old Macdonald is very much at the mercy of the wind.

demonstrating innovative ways of creating interesting golf in inhospitable landscapes. Beyond Las Vegas, Mesquite's spectacular Wolf Creek[30] is blasted through a rocky moonscape while Jack Nicklaus's Montreux G and CC[31] – a regular stop on the PGA tour – is the highest-rated course in the Reno area.

NEW BOOM AREAS

The Pacific north-west was, for many decades, somewhat quiet golfing country, but recent resort and real-estate development in Oregon has lifted the region's profile. The Bend/Sunriver area in central Oregon has gained a prominent foothold in this regard, but the region's superstar, without question, lies along the coast, where the Bandon Dunes[32] golf resort offers some first-rate courses including Tom Doak's Pacific Dunes, David McLay Kidd's Bandon Dunes, Bill Coore and

Ben Crenshaw's Bandon Trails and Doak and Jim Urbino's Old Macdonald[33].

Outside the contiguous 48 states, Alaska is predictably devoid of outstanding golf, but the resort capital of Hawaii is the polar opposite. A 1926 visit by Seth Raynor – who planned much-altered layouts at PGA Tour stop Waialae[34] and Mid-Pacific[35] – gave the islands a solid start, but it has been primarily through modern resort development that the game has boomed.

On the Big Island, Robert Trent Jones Snr's Mauna Kea[36] and Mauna Lani[37] lead the way, while Maui offers Kapalua[38], where Bill Coore and Ben Crenshaw's spectacular Plantation Course annually entertains the Tour professionals. Kauai, for its part, features notable Robert Trent Jones Jnr designs at the Princeville Resort[39] (45 holes) and at Poipu Bay[40] – annual site of the PGA's Grand Slam of Golf.

Mauna Kea's much photographed 3rd hole has recently been extended to a 272-yard par three, all carry over the ocean!

Shadow Creek
North Las Vegas, Nevada

The veritable mantra of architect Tom Fazio, 'total site manipulation' was more than a design theory at Shadow Creek; it was an absolute necessity. But Shadow Creek was funded by casino mogul Steve Wynn, who could well afford such extravagance.

Shadow Creek
North Las Vegas, Nevada

Designers: Tom Fazio & Steve Wynn, 1989

In a modern era in which the majority of potentially great golf-course sites are either exhausted or too environmentally encumbered for profitable development, Tom Fazio has established himself as a designer unfazed by starting with less. Moving massive amounts of earth and engaging in 'total site manipulation', he has successfully created well-known courses in barren deserts, abandoned quarries and hilly mountain sites, all neatly framed to look as aesthetically appealing as possible. Although such large-scale projects often lack the subtle, more intricate contouring associated with courses laid more gently into the land, they have certainly served Fazio well, for there has been no bigger name in the design business since the 1980s.

GOLFING OASIS

Such qualifications surely made Tom Fazio an ideal candidate when, during the mid-1980s, Las

'Shadow Creek was supposed to excite one's emotions, and then test one's golf. It wasn't designed to be the hardest test in America.'
STEVE WYNN

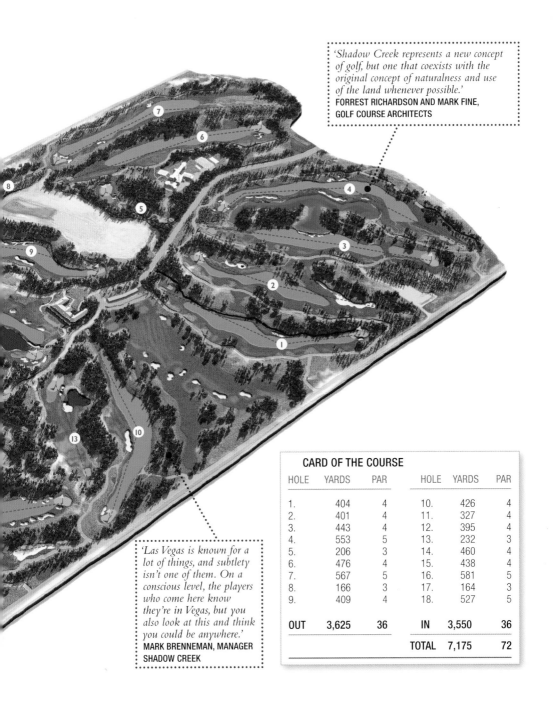

'Shadow Creek represents a new concept of golf, but one that coexists with the original concept of naturalness and use of the land whenever possible.'
FORREST RICHARDSON AND MARK FINE, GOLF COURSE ARCHITECTS

'Las Vegas is known for a lot of things, and subtlety isn't one of them. On a conscious level, the players who come here know they're in Vegas, but you also look at this and think you could be anywhere.'
MARK BRENNEMAN, MANAGER SHADOW CREEK

CARD OF THE COURSE

HOLE	YARDS	PAR	HOLE	YARDS	PAR
1.	404	4	10.	426	4
2.	401	4	11.	327	4
3.	443	4	12.	395	4
4.	553	5	13.	232	3
5.	206	3	14.	460	4
6.	476	4	15.	438	4
7.	567	5	16.	581	5
8.	166	3	17.	164	3
9.	409	4	18.	527	5
OUT	**3,625**	**36**	**IN**	**3,550**	**36**
			TOTAL	**7,175**	**72**

Vegas magnate Steve Wynn decided to build a golf course. With his then-trademark property perhaps fittingly called The Mirage, Wynn was experienced in creating something from nothing in the middle of the Nevada desert. Furthermore, as an avid golfer, he had clear ideas as to just what type of facility he desired – so much so, in fact, that Fazio himself willingly acknowledged Wynn as a co-designer when the project ultimately came to fruition.

In many ways Shadow Creek represents the modern equivalent of Charles Blair Macdonald and Seth Raynor's long-lost Lido Golf Club, a 1917 New York creation in which more than 2 million cubic yards of landfill were utilized to reclaim a previously underwater site, effectively allowing the designers to shape the landscape to their every whim. In suburban Las Vegas, reclaiming land was hardly an issue; finding more than the faintest amount of natural contour within it was. The result was an excavation of earth massive enough not only to create the desired playing surface (plus numerous water hazards) but also to build what amounted to a giant berm around the perimeter, nicely secluding the course and also limiting the player's external view to the tops of the surrounding mountains rather than the less-attractive desert below.

STEVE WYNN'S IDEAS

Given this blank canvas, Wynn could have patterned the course's aesthetic after any inland region or style, and he chose the sand-hills region of North Carolina. To this end, more than 21,000 mature trees were imported and their environs surrounded by pine needles, as well as pampas and other non-native grasses. Wynn also copied Augusta National by minimizing rough and dictating that where it was absolutely necessary, it should be closely groomed and minimally punishing. He also required the course to be

walkable, and that its vistas – over which the designers obviously held complete control – be shaped with the perspective of the walker in mind.

As a final unique point, Wynn and Fazio followed the old-fashioned method of designing nearly every hole in the field rather than working from a set of office-drawn plans. This perhaps explains why Shadow Creek offers a bit more panache than many more office-born projects.

MAN-MADE SPLENDOUR

Following a fine 404-yard opener, where the startlingly natural-looking Shadow Creek flanks the entire left side, and the 401-yard 2nd, things come alive at the 443-yard 3rd. This is a long two-shotter with an approach played uphill to a large green that, though unbunkered, falls away at its front and right edges. The 553-yard 4th sweeps leftwards around a lake before players cross the entrance road to challenge the 'abyss' at the exciting 206-yard 5th. A solid enough par three based solely on its length, this hole features the one hazard specifically demanded by Wynn: a 60-foot deep, tree-filled chasm, which must be carried (with only a small left-side safety area) if the putting surface is to be reached.

The front nine's second par three, the 166-yard 8th, also relies heavily on oversized contouring. It is built into its own secluded valley accessed by a pair of tunnels: one by the tee, the other by the green. Then the outward half closes with the 409-yard 9th, a straight par four on which the creek returns, flanking the left side of the driving area before angling short and left of the green.

The back nine is best known for its big finish, although that stretch could be said to start at the 13th, a downhill 232-yarder played to a suitably large green slanting rightwards, beyond sand and a water-filled ravine. Both the 14th and 15th are long par fours with greens flanked by a lake and creek respectively, while the 581-yard 16th, comfortably the Shadow Creek's longest hole, doglegs right, then crosses tumbling terrain before climbing to a narrow, elevated green.

ENLIGHTENED EXTRAVAGANCE

The 17th is the club's shortest and most-photographed hole, measuring a mere 164 yards – but it is nearly all-carry to a tiny, pond-fronted green set before a high, forested ridge and a large waterfall. The entire setting, though functional enough, is patently over-the-top in the middle of a desert. But first-class showman that he is, Wynn understood the delicate balance. 'Had we delivered this kind of treatment too often, it might have been excessive. But it was irresistible to do it once,' he wrote of the 17th. Though a touch less fancy,

the 527-yard finishing hole is comparably exciting; it is lined by a series of ponds and is eminently reachable in two provided the golfer is prepared for long water carries on each swing.

NOW OPEN TO THE PUBLIC

During Shadow Creek's early years, Wynn lived in a mansion off the 18th fairway and reserved the course for his friends and select clients, but in 2000 he lost the property to Kirk Kirkorian's MGM Grand Resorts in a hostile takeover. Today the golf course can be accessed, for a hefty fee, by guests of Kirkorian's properties. Tom Fazio's finest work, then, has become the world's most expensive public golf course, but the sheer magnitude of its creation remains plainly apparent for all to see.

Looking up the fairway at the 9th, it is difficult to believe that Shadow Creek was manufactured out of the Las Vegas desert.

Pacific Dunes
Bandon Resort, Oregon

Mike Keiser, owner of Bandon Resort, gave Tom Doak instructions for Pacific Dunes that every architect longs for: 'Find the best course you can and without allowances for houses or golf-cart paths as there will be neither. This will be a walking-only course, free of outside disturbances.'

Bandon Dunes Golf Resort (Pacific Dunes)
Bandon Resort, Oregon

Designer: Tom Doak, 2001
Major events: Curtis Cup 2006

Following the immediate success of David McLay Kidd's Bandon Dunes – the first course at Bandon Resort – Tom Doak was commissioned to build Pacific Dunes on land to the north of Bandon Dunes. The terrain was quite diverse, highlighted

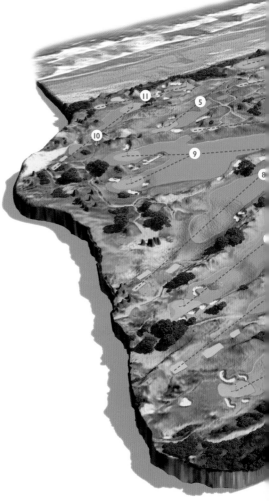

CARD OF THE COURSE

HOLE	YARDS	PAR	HOLE	YARDS	PAR
1.	370	4	10.	206	3
2.	368	4	11.	148	3
3.	499	5	12.	529	5
4.	463	4	13.	444	4
5.	199	3	14.	145	3
6.	316	4	15.	539	5
7.	464	4	16.	338	4
8.	400	4	17.	208	3
9.	406	4	18.	591	5
OUT	**3,485**	**36**	**IN**	**3,148**	**35**
			TOTAL	**6,633**	**71**

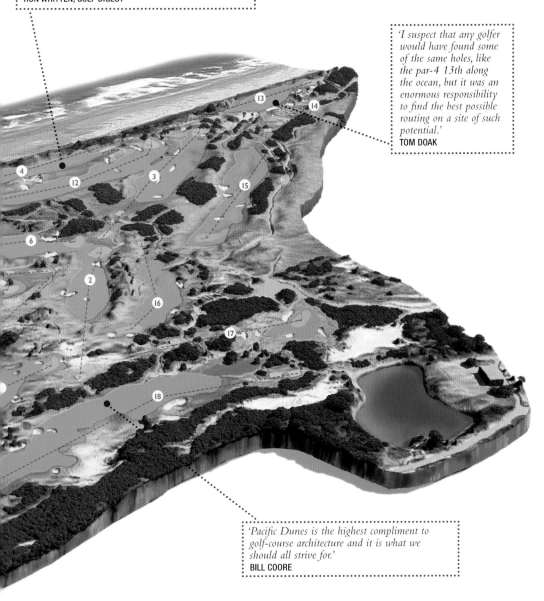

'Pacific Dunes...emerges as perhaps the last great meeting of sand and sea on American soil.'
RON WHITTEN, GOLF DIGEST

'I suspect that any golfer would have found some of the same holes, like the par-4 13th along the ocean, but it was an enormous responsibility to find the best possible routing on a site of such potential.'
TOM DOAK

'Pacific Dunes is the highest compliment to golf-course architecture and it is what we should all strive for.'
BILL COORE

by the spectacular cliff line with the Pacific Ocean pounding below. To the east, there was an enormous valley where the 17th and 18th holes now are. In between the cliff and the valley, there was a gorse plain and a large sandy bowl area.

FUN GOLF

Having travelled together in the United Kingdom, Mike Keiser and Doak admired the rugged naturalness of Royal County Down as well as the routing at Royal Portrush, where each nine reaches to the edges of the cliffs. Armed with this knowledge and free of the restrictions that hamper most modern courses, Doak created a course that Keiser cherished – one that catered for fun golf.

Notionally, it might be assumed that fun golf is what every owner likes. After all, golf is a game

meant to be enjoyed. However, after the Second World War and the Vietnam War, numerous courses built in the United States were long, arduous tests, reflecting in some ways the mood of the nation.

The pressure was now on Doak to build a great course. Fortunately, relying on his encyclopedic knowledge from having studied more than 900 courses worldwide, Doak was able to employ features possessed by some world-class courses.

NATURAL CONTOURS

On the 370-yard 1st, the crumpled fairway, complete with its humps and bumps, stands in stark contrast to the fairways of most modern courses where heavy machinery flattens the natural contours. The 368-yard 2nd hole is multiroute due to a central bunker in the fairway. Into the

Doak considers the 13th to be the most natural hole at Pacific Dunes, hemmed in by the cliff line and a large sand blow-out.

prevailing northerly, the golfer has to think long and hard about carrying it and reaching the lower level of the fairway from where the green opens up. Such a central hazard had all but vanished from American golf architecture during the period from 1960 to 1995.

As highlighted for over a century by the Old Course at St Andrews, central bunkers create multiple playing routes within holes. Golfers must decide which option is best for them, based on their own swing that day as well as the wind and the day's hole location. Most modern golf-course architects had sadly ignored this tenet of course design, frequently pushing bunkers to the sides of holes where they only punish a wayward shot. However, Doak's designs differ from those of his peers in that he featured classic design elements

such as central bunkering throughout his courses. At Pacific Dunes, the golfer appreciates this fact again when standing on the 3rd tee, where he has a clear view of two massive central bunkers in the fairway.

Ever sensitive to the desires of the retail golfer (as he calls recreational golfers), Keiser was delighted when Doak's routing ran the 463-yard 4th along the edge of the 100-foot tall cliff. Most golfers travel great distances to reach the Bandon Resort, and it is spectacular, one-of-a-kind moments such as this one that make them glad they did so.

Though it moves inland for the rest of the front nine, the course continues without let-up. The 199-yard 5th green nestled in the dunes accepts balls that kick in from its high left side. This is but

A treacherous bunker protects the right side of the 3rd green. Its exposure to the wind makes distance judgment testing.

one example of the course's short-game interest and it is also a prime example of the superb turf conditions that the greenkeeping staff presents. With its cool evenings, rainfall, sandy soil and fescue grasses, Pacific Dunes and the other Bandon courses play akin to the links in the United Kingdom. Players with the talent to play the ball low and under the wind relish the opportunity to use their full shot-making repertoire.

A PAR FOUR TO TREASURE

Tom Doak's favourite courses, including St Andrews, Royal Melbourne and Crystal Downs, share a common trait of great, short two-shotters. At the 316-yard 6th, Doak created one that any course would proudly call its own. The 7th green complex is a prime example of the architect following nature's lead. According to Doak, the 'bunkers to the left of the green are formalized

the high side of the central front bunker can be gathered close to the hole.

FOLLOWING NATURE'S LEAD

For six holes from the turn, the golfer faces only one par-four hole and that is at the 13th. This unconventional sequencing of holes was not lightly settled on. Yes, the 206-yard 10th and 148-yard 11th are back-to-back par threes. However, the downhill 10th is bunkerless to a large green with subtle rolls level with its surroundings, while the 11th is the opposite: its elevated green set into the dunescape is surrounded by bunkers, making it the smallest target on the course. Ultimately, the compelling nature of each of these holes convinced Doak and Keiser that they were the best sequence for that course. Both men believed in following the natural contours and knew it was nonsensical to think that all terrain should yield nines with two par threes, two par fives and five par fours. They appreciated the unconventional aspects of some of the world's great courses. For example, Alister MacKenzie featured back-to-back par threes, par fives and short par fours at Cypress Point.

Doak's 15th green complex with its plateau green offers the golfer the same approach options as the famed Foxy hole at Royal Dornoch, one of Keiser's favourite holes. A classic drive-and-pitch hole follows, this time with the general playing angles of the famous 10th at Riviera.

Against a stunning, gorse-covered dune as a backdrop, traditionalists embrace the Redan-playing characteristics of the 208-yard 17th as they feed the ball in from high right. Typical of the rest of the holes, the golfer is given plenty of room to work the ball. Indeed, the diversity of the challenge at Pacific Dunes combined with its freedom to create shots are at the heart of what makes it so enjoyable to play.

versions of natural blowouts and the dips and mounds short of the green have never been touched by equipment'.

In beautiful contrast to the table-top 7th green is the green at the 400-yard 8th, with its punchbowl right half inspired by Doak's affection for the 3rd hole at Woking. When the hole location is right, approach shots that skirt around

The Olympic Club
San Francisco, California

When a newly formed club chooses to call itself Knollwood, Silver Oaks or even the TPC Death Valley, the flatly generic ring does little to suggest that any sort of special experience lies in the offing. But when an organization christens itself The Olympic Club, surely that must suggest greater prospects altogether.

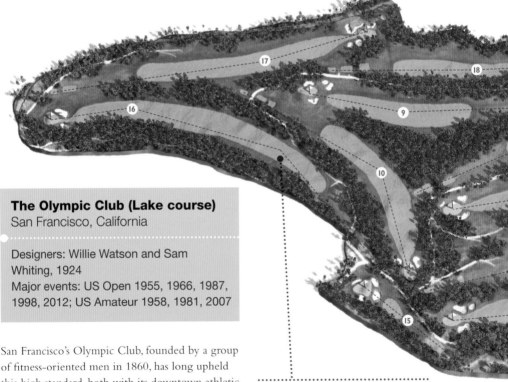

The Olympic Club (Lake course)
San Francisco, California

Designers: Willie Watson and Sam Whiting, 1924
Major events: US Open 1955, 1966, 1987, 1998, 2012; US Amateur 1958, 1981, 2007

San Francisco's Olympic Club, founded by a group of fitness-oriented men in 1860, has long upheld this high standard, both with its downtown athletic club and its coastal golfing facility. The latter is situated on high ground above the Pacific, just across Lake Merced from Harding Park.

'I never really wrapped my mind about winning, the place is so demanding, and so all I was really concerned about was keeping the ball in front of me.'
WEBB SIMPSON, 2012 US OPEN CHAMPION

BEGINNINGS

Golf actually began on this site in 1917, when an organization known as the Lakeside Golf and Country Club opened a short-lived 6,410-yard Wilfrid Reid-designed course. The expanding Olympians purchased the Lakeside Club shortly after the First World War and quickly hired Scottish émigré Willie Watson to redesign it. Enlisting the club's future greenkeeper, Sam Whiting, as his assistant, Watson proceeded to create a pair of 18-hole courses, the 6,606-yard

CARD OF THE COURSE

HOLE	YARDS	PAR	HOLE	YARDS	PAR
1.	520	4	10.	424	4
2.	428	4	11.	430	4
3.	247	3	12.	451	4
4.	438	4	13.	199	3
5.	498	4	14.	419	4
6.	489	4	15.	154	3
7.	288	4	16.	670	5
8.	200	3	17.	522	5
9.	449	4	18.	344	4
OUT	3,557	34	IN	3,613	36
			TOTAL	7,170	70

'In the 2012 US Open the 6th hole proved hardest against par, averaging 4.54.'

'This golf course is just so demanding that a fraction off you pay the price.'
TIGER WOODS

A view of the downhill 247-yard 3rd. Few holes in the world better balance a championship-calibre test with great scenery.

Ocean Course (which included several spectacular holes on the coastal side of Skyline Boulevard) and the 6,589-yard Lake Course. Not surprisingly, it was the flashier Ocean that was the club's initial attraction – that is, until a series of early landslides claimed several of its showpiece holes, leading to a complete Whiting redesign in 1927.

Even with the Ocean Course relegated to a shorter, awkwardly configured status, it took a good 20 years for the Lake Course to reach a position of golfing prominence. It initially occupied a semi-barren hillside, was devoid of water hazards and out-of-bounds, and included only a single fairway bunker. Whiting addressed these issues by undertaking one of golf's grandest-ever tree planting projects, a comprehensive endeavour that

added more than 30,000 pine, cypress, eucalyptus and palms to the mix. As a result, by the end of the Second World War, the Lake Course became one of the game's most demanding tests, the gnarled limbs that tightly frame its every fairway requiring an unceasing level of accuracy rarely matched in championship golf.

But if trees have succeeded in turning a relatively basic design into a test difficult enough to host US Opens, so too have they given it a distinctively beautiful atmosphere. For a game at the Lake Course is an aesthetically enriching experience, its massive walls of green secluding every fairway, standing tall amid San Francisco's frequent fog, and occasionally opening to marvellous views of the adjacent Lake Merced and the distant Golden Gate Bridge. What the Lake Course lacks in strategic design, then, it certainly compensates for in difficulty and character.

NEGOTIATING THE TREES

Many of the Lake's more interesting holes fall on the outward half, with few capturing the layout's challenge and ambience as well as the 247-yard 3rd. Playing from a substantially elevated tee, it is a downhill one-shotter aimed at a narrow green pinched, both at its edges and in its approach, by four prominent bunkers. The target itself is daunting, while the view above the treeline – across much of the city's western expanse towards the Golden Gate and the Marin Headlands – is nothing short of inspiring.

Should a golfer still not grasp the true difficulty, the course sets a sterner test at the 4th and 5th – a pair of longer par fours (438 and 498 yards respectively) frequently rated among the toughest back-to-back holes in golf. Here a player faces the classic Olympic Club challenge, for neither hole has a fairway bunker nor, strictly speaking, bunkering that closely guards its putting surface. Both are extremely difficult driving holes, with fairways curving awkwardly against sloping terrain and tree limbs reaching out to snare even marginally wayward shots. The temptation to use a fairway metal is huge, but if accomplished safely such a tactic results in much longer-than-desired approaches.

The Lake is the odd course comprised of a front eight and back 10, for it is indeed the recently-lengthened 200-yard 8th, with its small, bunker-ringed green, that returns to the base of the huge hill-top clubhouse. From here a run of mid-length par fours, plus a pair of shortish par threes, carry play first to the property's northern tip, then back, alongside John Muir Drive, to a somewhat offbeat set of finishers.

CLOSERS

The 670-yard 16th is an obvious bruiser, making what seems an endless left turn to a very small, tightly bunkered green. Amazingly, it was actually reached in two by the legendary Bobby Jones in 1929, though it is worth noting that the forest that blockades the inside of the dogleg today did not yet exist at the time and the hole was also somewhat shorter.

For US Open play, the 522-yard 17th used to be converted to a bruising par four, though with its sharply sidehill fairway and conspicuously undersized green, it is seldom confused with the fairest of two-shotters. The 18th, on the other hand, seems a perfect closer for so quirky a course. It is a tricky 344-yard drive-and-pitch played downhill to a narrow fairway, then up to a dangerously pitched green built into the slopes below the clubhouse.

THE LONGEST 7,170 YARDS IN GOLF

Olympic has hosted US Opens since the 1950s, though the men who lost those events – Ben Hogan, Arnold Palmer and Tom Watson – are better remembered than their winners, Jack Fleck, Billy Casper and Scott Simpson.

Still, with its heavy seaside air, lush, sloping fairways and enough narrowness to make even the best players favour fairway metals off many tees, Olympic is likely to remain the longest-playing 7,170 yards in golf, averaging 73.8 strokes per round during the 2012 US Open. Olympic Lake is also that rare Golden Age course, which, despite few design changes of consequence, actually poses more of a challenge to the world's best today than it did in its infancy. Such a recipe is likely to keep it tournament prominent for decades to come.

Pebble Beach
Pebble Beach, California

The 19th-century novelist Robert Louis Stevenson once wrote that California's Monterey Peninsula was 'the finest meeting of land and sea in the world'. But for golfers his words have long been narrowed to describe the area's centrepiece, the Pebble Beach Golf Links, which occupies one of the most spectacular golfing shorelines of any course on earth.

Pebble Beach Golf Links
Pebble Beach, California

Designers: Douglas Grant and Jack Neville, 1919 and H. Chandler Egan, 1928
Major events: US Open 1972, 1982, 1992, 2000, 2010; USPGA 1977; US Amateur 1929, 1947, 1961, 1999; US Women's Amateur 1940, 1948

Pebble Beach was built primarily as a promotional device by Samuel Morse, president of the then-fledgling Del Monte Properties Company. Much has been made of Morse's selection of golf course architects, a pair of 'unknowns' named Jack Neville and Douglas Grant. Morse's first choice was Charles Blair Macdonald (who reportedly turned down all entreaties to make the long journey west) and Morse was apparently of the erroneous belief that Donald Ross

The English architect, Herbert Fowler, is credited with creating this back tee for the 18th hole, making it a dramatic and famous hole.

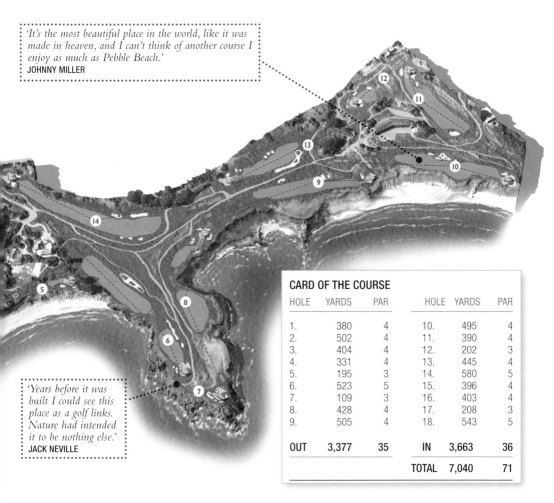

CARD OF THE COURSE

HOLE	YARDS	PAR	HOLE	YARDS	PAR
1.	380	4	10.	495	4
2.	502	4	11.	390	4
3.	404	4	12.	202	3
4.	331	4	13.	445	4
5.	195	3	14.	580	5
6.	523	5	15.	396	4
7.	109	3	16.	403	4
8.	428	4	17.	208	3
9.	505	4	18.	543	5
OUT	3,377	35	IN	3,663	36
			TOTAL	7,040	71

had returned to the United Kingdom to serve in the First World War. A.W. Tillinghast, Dr Alister MacKenzie and William Flynn were still largely unknown west of the Mississippi, and Morse was under considerable financial pressure at the time of the course's construction, so the notion of hiring a pair of amateurs – who, under USGA rules, could not be compensated financially for their work – actually made perfect sense. Neville and

Grant's original design might well be described as the skeleton around which the modern Pebble Beach layout has filled out, for it followed virtually the same routing but featured far less sand, smaller greens and a back-tee yardage of only 6,107.

A MAJOR RENOVATION

When the US Amateur was awarded to Pebble Beach in 1929, a two-time winner of the event,

The cliff-top 10th, where a drive played close to this fairway
bunker leaves the ideal approach.

H. Chandler Egan, was hired to bring the scenic-but-diminutive course up to national championship standard. Egan was not alone in performing 1920s alterations at Pebble Beach, for the extension of the then-325-yard 18th to world-renowned par-five status was done by British architect Herbert Fowler in 1921, while the rebuilding of the 8th and 13th greens was directed by Dr Alister MacKenzie during his 1928 construction of nearby Cypress Point.

UNIQUELY SPECTACULAR GOLF

Though some of its inland holes may not be quite as thrilling as those along the water, Pebble Beach today stands as one of golf's greatest playing experiences, its figure-of-eight routing leading golfers to the cliff tops from the 4th tee through the 10th green, then back again at the 17th and 18th.

The skilled player knows that he or she must come out firing, for the greatest opportunities to score are found over the first six holes. The 502-yard 2nd provides such a chance. Despite a deep cross-bunker 75 yards shy of the putting surface and more sand recently added on the left side of the driving area, it is often reachable in two and thus a real birdie opportunity – except when the USGA converts it to a par four, as they now do during regular US Open visits. During the 2012 Open this hole played as the second hardest on the course.

A NEW 5TH

For the better part of eight decades, the 5th was an inland par three, unavoidably routed through the trees because Samuel Morse had sold the adjacent oceanfront land shortly before selecting the site for his golf course. It was replaced by the present Jack Nicklaus-designed 195-yarder in 1998.

The last of the early scoring holes, the 6th runs downhill to a fairway guarded left by a huge bunker and right by Stillwater Cove. Its small green is usually reachable in two by better players, but the second shot must be carried across a corner of the cove to a steeply elevated headland.

RENOWNED CLIFF-TOP HOLES

The 109-yard 7th is among the most photographed holes in golf, and with good reason. Set at the tip of the headland, exposed to the Pacific elements, its downhill tee shot can range from half a pitch to a full mid-iron, depending entirely on the wind. As scenic a test as the game can offer, it is, quite simply, one of golf's defining holes.

The golfer now reaches what is widely considered Pebble Beach's hardest stretch, for the 8th, 9th and 10th are all cliff-top par fours of major challenge and worldwide distinction. The 8th is the shortest of them, but the forced lay-up required on its tee shot results in a disproportionately long second. This approach highlights another of Pebble Beach's legendary images, for it is played across a deep, ocean-filled chasm to Alister MacKenzie's sharply sloping green, which sits just above the cliff top, menaced by bunkers long and short.

Probably the most difficult hole on the course, the 9th follows the coastline but not too tightly. The fairway slopes heavily from left to right, frequently resulting in hanging lies for what amounts to one of golf's toughest long-iron approaches. The green seems a bit too small for its purpose, and is guarded front-left by a particularly deep bunker and right by a rugged, iceplant-filled slope to the beach.

The last of this dangerous trio, and arguably Pebble Beach's toughest driving hole, the 10th offers little room for error – its sloping fairway being pinched by sand left and the ocean right. The approach comes from another hanging lie, this time to a green tucked behind a cliffside crevice and nearly ringed by sand, with the wide crescent

Scene of agony and ecstasy in several US Opens, the 17th green (described in detail opposite).

of Carmel Beach serving as an attractive backdrop. From here the routing moves inland to a stretch of holes that are solid, but a touch less exciting and far less romantic.

WORLD'S MOST FAMOUS FINISHER

With the possible exception of St Andrews, it is doubtful that any golf course has a more illustrious pair of finishers than Pebble Beach, beginning with the treacherous par-three 17th. This unique one-shotter features a terribly narrow green resembling a tilted hourglass, its two halves clearly divided by a prominent ridge. The entire front of

the putting surface is protected by a single huge bunker while seven smaller hazards flank the back.

Perhaps not the game's finest finisher architecturally but likely its most scenic, the 18th is played from a promontory tee, the drive daring the golfer to skirt the rocky coastline. With the prevailing wind blowing against, most second shots will be placed safely right of the long bunker and sea wall.

With its small, heavily pitched greens, strong coastal winds and plethora of thrilling holes, Pebble Beach remains rigorous enough to challenge the world's best.

TRIUMPH AND HEARTBREAK FOR NICKLAUS
PEBBLE BEACH'S FAMOUS 17TH

Jack Nicklaus has called Pebble Beach his favourite golf course, hardly surprising given that he has won both a US Amateur (1961) and a US Open (1972) there. But rarely has a single hole represented such high and low points of a single man's career as has Pebble Beach's 17th for Nicklaus. In 1972, he stood on the 71st tee with the wind blowing and the outcome still very much in doubt. From 218 yards away, he laced one of history's great 1-irons, a low, wind-cheating bullet that hit the base of the flagstick and stopped only inches away, thus clinching the title.

Ten years later, however, it would be an altogether different story. Already in the clubhouse with a four-under-par total of 284, Nicklaus looked a likely US Open winner when

Tom Watson arrived at the 71st tied for the lead, then hooked a 2-iron into some nasty greenside rough. Confident that Watson would now do well just to force a Monday play-off, Nicklaus looked on as his arch-rival proceeded to hole one of the game's most memorable chips, then calmly birdie the par-five 18th, ending Nicklaus's last great chance to capture a record fifth Open title.

Cypress Point
Pebble Beach, California

Residing at the top of any list of golf's most magical spots, the Cypress Point Club has stood synonymous with both superior design and sublime, other-worldly beauty since its opening in August 1928.

Cypress Point Club
Pebble Beach, California

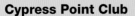

Designers: Dr Alister MacKenzie and Robert Hunter, 1928
Major events: Walker Cup 1981

'No golf architect was more endowed with natural features of his work than Alister MacKenzie at Cypress Point – majestic woodlands, a hint of heathland here and there and the savage nobility of the coast made for unforgettable holes.'
PAT WARD-THOMAS

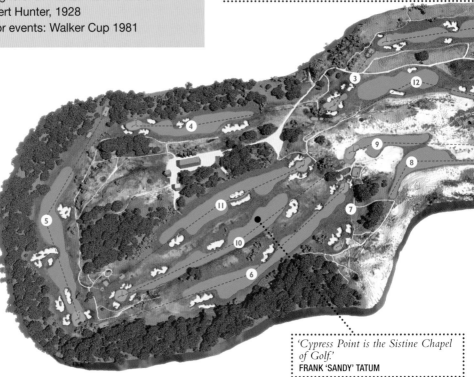

'Cypress Point is the Sistine Chapel of Golf.'
FRANK 'SANDY' TATUM

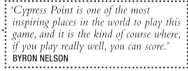

What if a golf course could be built on terrain
so beautifully varied as to incorporate a rocky,
beach-strewn coastline, massive silver-white
sand dunes and lush forests as lovely as
any national park? This is not a rhetorical
question, because the game has been
blessed with a single exemplary answer –
Cypress Point.

It was the brainchild of the 1921
US Women's Amateur champion Marion
Hollins. A New Yorker by birth, Hollins had
already created Long Island's novel Women's
National Golf and Tennis Club (today's
Glen Head Country Club) before moving west
in 1923. There she soon carved a successful niche
for herself in the real-estate division of Samuel
Morse's Del Monte Properties Company.

HIRING DR MACKENZIE

Cypress Point is widely viewed as the defining
point of the great Dr Alister MacKenzie's design
career, yet he was not, in fact, Hollins's first choice.
That honour went to Seth Raynor, who had been
consultant on the Women's National design and
builder of gems such as Fishers Island, Shoreacres
and Yale. Raynor's mandate was to build not just
Cypress Point but also two more courses at the
nearby Monterey Peninsula Country Club as part
of Morse's grand scheme. Unfortunately, Raynor
died in 1926 having only partially completed one
of the two Monterey layouts. But at Cypress Point,
the matchless property and the involvement of

CARD OF THE COURSE

HOLE	YARDS	PAR	HOLE	YARDS	PAR
1.	421	4	10.	480	5
2.	548	5	11.	437	4
3.	162	3	12.	404	4
4.	384	4	13.	365	4
5.	493	5	14.	388	4
6.	518	5	15.	143	3
7.	168	3	16.	231	3
8.	363	4	17.	393	4
9.	292	4	18.	346	4
OUT	**3,349**	**37**	**IN**	**3,187**	**35**
			TOTAL	**6,536**	**72**

A view of the 16th green and, beyond it, the 17th tee, which plays across the ocean to the fairway mid-left of the picture.

some big-name founders necessitated the project continuing and quickly, so Hollins turned to Alister MacKenzie.

MACKENZIE'S OBJECTIVES

On taking over the Cypress Point project, MacKenzie opted to discard all previous plans and instead devised his own routing that had to accomplish three key objectives. First, the finishers were to be placed near to, or directly alongside, the ocean, creating a closing run universally ranked among the world's most dramatic. Secondly, holes were to be woven in and out of the dunes and forest throughout the round, giving the layout an adventurous, ever-changing feel. And finally, MacKenzie's routing succeeded in utilizing a single huge sand dune as an attractive backdrop for no fewer than four holes (the 3rd, 6th, 9th and 11th), a splendidly efficient adaptation of form to function.

The peripatetic Alister MacKenzie left Cypress Point's construction under the watchful eye of his western partner, the noted Socialist, Robert Hunter. It is difficult to say what role, if any, Hunter played in the actual design process, but, whatever the creative balance of power, MacKenzie was pleased enough with the results to draw pre-opening comparisons with St Andrews. 'For years I have been contending that in our generation no other golf course could possibly compete with the strategic problems, the thrills, excitement, variety and lasting and increasing interest of the Old course', MacKenzie wrote, 'but the completion of Cypress Point has made me change my mind.'

THE OPENERS

Cypress Point opens with a tee shot across Seventeen Mile Drive, and immediately

MacKenzie has the golfer thinking: is it possible to carry the cypresses that cluster on the right side some 230 yards down the fairway or would it be safer to play away to the longer left side? Regardless of choice, with the ocean tumbling into nearby Fan Shell Beach and the slightly elevated green framed by a massive backdrop of silvery dunes, players know immediately that they are indeed entering hallowed golfing ground.

The 2nd moves across the top of a long ridge, its right side flanked by out-of-bounds, its left by a hillside falling into deep, wild grass. The 3rd plays to the base of the large central sand dune, and then it is off into the forest at the 4th.

MacKenzie demonstrated his willingness to buck architectural convention by building back-to-back par fives at the 5th and 6th. The former, at only 493 yards, an eminently reachable dogleg left, while the 6th drive is of interest, because the golfer must flirt with a pair of right-side bunkers in order to gain an ideal second-shot angle and a favourable slope.

The 292-yard 9th remains one of the world's elite sub-300-yard par fours. Its narrow fairway is surrounded by sand, and its long, terrifically sloping green is set spectacularly into the northern face of MacKenzie's ever-present central dune.

AESTHETIC PERFECTION

Beginning a run of wonderful par fours is the 11th. Here a pair of centre-line bunkers invades the fairway beginning at the 275-yard mark, typically calling for a laid-up tee shot, and thus a fairly long approach to the last of the greens positioned beneath the dune. On the other hand, the 12th requires a long left-to-right drive to skirt dangerous ground in order to find the optimum approach angle to a small, elevated green. Most famous among this quartet is the 13th, with its impressive backdrop of the Pacific and Fan Shell

Beach. Finally, the 14th features clumps of mature cypress trees, which narrow the fairway severely from 265 yards.

LA CRÈME DE LA CRÈME

Ranking among the game's best-known short par threes, the 15th is played across a rocky Pacific inlet from a tee balanced on an exposed headland. The green is a wildly shaped affair, with narrow extensions at both its front and far right inviting numerous fascinating pin placements, and six magnificently sculpted bunkers providing danger and some wonderful artistic definition.

An oceanside walk through the cypresses brings the golfer to one of the greatest and most spectacular golf holes ever built – the breathtaking 231-yard 16th. Interestingly, MacKenzie initially planned this legendary one-shotter to be a short par four, later crediting Marion Hollins with convincing him otherwise. Played across a broad, rocky bay, it requires a direct carry of nearly 220 windswept yards to reach the putting surface. However, it also offers the faint of heart a wide stretch of left-side fairway on which to play safe. With its bunker-ringed green occupying the beginning of a huge, rocky headland, the 16th represents the finest blend of challenge, beauty, strategy and simple, jaw-dropping awe in the history of the game.

Remarkably, the 17th measures up almost equally in this regard. Its drive rates among the most thrilling anywhere, played across another vast bay to an angled fairway nestled above a daunting bulwark of rock. A clump of cypresses springs up in the right-centre of the fairway at 275 yards. Today, these cypresses serve to threaten longer tee shots and impede the view of the approach, which, played to a green angling out onto one final promontory, is not easy to play, especially in a high wind.

Spyglass Hill
Pebble Beach, California

From a portfolio that once regularly boasted at least a dozen courses widely rated among America's top 100, Robert Trent Jones Snr's course at Spyglass Hill today remains the best of only a handful still regularly considered for such honours.

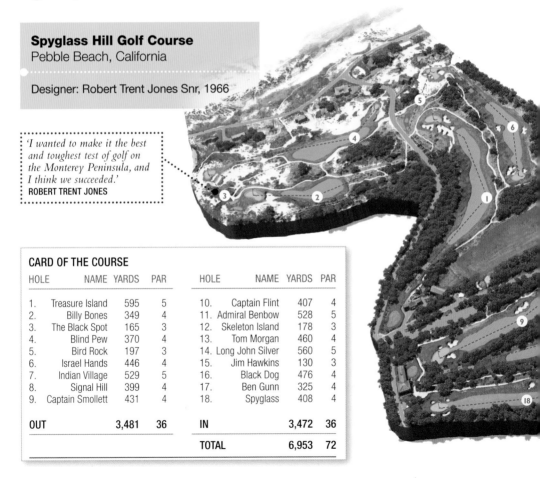

Spyglass Hill Golf Course
Pebble Beach, California

Designer: Robert Trent Jones Snr, 1966

> 'I wanted to make it the best and toughest test of golf on the Monterey Peninsula, and I think we succeeded.'
> **ROBERT TRENT JONES**

CARD OF THE COURSE

HOLE	NAME	YARDS	PAR	HOLE	NAME	YARDS	PAR
1.	Treasure Island	595	5	10.	Captain Flint	407	4
2.	Billy Bones	349	4	11.	Admiral Benbow	528	5
3.	The Black Spot	165	3	12.	Skeleton Island	178	3
4.	Blind Pew	370	4	13.	Tom Morgan	460	4
5.	Bird Rock	197	3	14.	Long John Silver	560	5
6.	Israel Hands	446	4	15.	Jim Hawkins	130	3
7.	Indian Village	529	5	16.	Black Dog	476	4
8.	Signal Hill	399	4	17.	Ben Gunn	325	4
9.	Captain Smollett	431	4	18.	Spyglass	408	4
OUT		**3,481**	**36**	**IN**		**3,472**	**36**
				TOTAL		**6,953**	**72**

For American golfers born after the First World War, no name is more synonymous with the field of golf course architecture than Robert Trent Jones Snr. A native of Ince, in Cheshire, England, Trent Jones emigrated to the United States as a youth before pursuing a self-designed college curriculum whose focus on agronomy, engineering and landscape architecture specifically prepared him for his chosen work. It was this expertise – combined with a dearth of postwar competition – that would eventually lead to an unmatched degree of worldwide industry dominance.

> *'Pebble and Cypress make you want to play golf, Spyglass Hill makes you want to go fishing.'*
> **JACK NICKLAUS**

AN ARCHITECTURAL PIONEER

Perhaps more importantly, Trent Jones single-handedly changed the architectural medium, leading it away from the strategic approach of the Golden Age towards what he called the 'Heroic' school of design: big, power-oriented layouts with copious bunkering, large, undulating greens and an overall degree of difficulty that he aptly summed up as 'a hard par or an easy bogey'. Trent Jones ultimately completed more than 450 global projects, performed redesign work on numerous Major championship sites and generally dominated his profession so extensively that half a generation of American architects began prominently using their own middle names in desperate attempts at keeping up.

What Trent Jones's work frequently lacked, however, was a polished aesthetic and a real degree of variety, with all too many holes amounting to long, nearly symmetrically bunkered tests largely interchangeable from site to site.

> *'Why is Spyglass Hill beautiful? Perhaps it's the sunlight that filters through the trees in the late afternoon while the deer graze and frolic, barely noticing a passing foursome. Or how time stands still as you walk in the morning mist down an empty fairway.'*
> **GIN PARK, HEAD PROFESSIONAL, SPYGLASS HILL**

Bunkers lie in wait for any weak approach shot on the 1st hole.

A REMARKABLE SETTING

Much of Spyglass Hill's lingering appeal lies in its great beauty. This is a golf course laid out amid a rare mix of glorious golfing backdrops: 13 of its holes cut through the Del Monte Forest – a stunningly green wonderland of gnarled cypress trees and tall California pines – while the remaining five tumble westwards towards the Pacific, breaching a splendid expanse of high, windblown sand dunes. In addition, Spyglass Hill bears the distinction of being, in many ways, rather an atypical Trent Jones design. It is not, for example, excessively long by contemporary standards (though its original 6,972 yards was certainly imposing enough in 1966); it features a number of interesting shorter holes; and its largely unbunkered driving areas offer the golfer a bit more room to manoeuvre than is found at courses such as Oakland Hills or Firestone. Yet despite such relative anomalies, Trent Jones still provided

a considerable dose of his architectural stock-in-trade: sheer, unmitigated toughness.

Tales of Spyglass Hill's terrors abound, particularly during its infancy when its putting surfaces (since remodelled) were exceedingly contoured and lightning quick. Teamed with timeless stalwarts Pebble Beach and Cypress Point as a tri-host of the then Bing Crosby Pro-Am, it was easily rated the toughest of the three courses by the professionals (who seldom even saw the back tees), particularly on the windiest of days when its north-westward exposure could occasionally make the dunes holes borderline unplayable.

Spyglass Hill was also, in those early years, the rare course to maintain a USGA rating above 76, which lead the Pulitzer Prize-winning sportswriter Jim Murray to call it 'a privateer plundering the golfing man' as well as 'a 300-acre unplayable lie'.

WHY THE DUNES?

From a design standpoint, students of golf architecture have long puzzled over why Trent Jones elected to begin, rather than end, his layout amid the dunes. The 1st is a colossal 595-yard par five that, though somewhat downhill, is no simple three-shotter. Its fairway is initially tree lined (demanding a straight first drive) before opening gently leftwards, towards the Pacific.

What follows is an exciting stretch of four shortish holes played at the complete mercy of the wind, beginning with the 349-yard 2nd, a drive-and-pitch whose approach climbs to a narrow, left-to-right sloping green nestled high amid the sand hills. The 165-yard 3rd then tumbles downhill with the Pacific as a scenic backdrop, while the 370-yard 4th is one of Trent Jones's more creative holes, a dogleg left played to an extremely narrow putting surface, which curls semi-blind behind a low-lying dune. Then the 197-yard 5th runs slightly uphill to a green guarded by a line of bunkers and a patch of the area's dreaded ice plant, before the tough, two-shot, 446-yard 6th climbs back into the forest.

INTO THE FOREST

It might be argued that the remainder of the layout is more 'typical' Trent Jones, with the par fours growing in stature, and the practice of excavating a pond in front of an otherwise nondescript green complex occurring on four occasions (it was five before a new-millennium renovation of the par-five 11th). But despite at least partially fitting these stereotypes, most of the inland holes are still quite appealing, in many cases simply because they achieve their difficulty without being saddled with overbearing length. Prime examples are a pair of shortish par threes considerably more engaging than any brutish 240-yard hole: the 178-yard 12th, played downhill

to a green angled right-to-left beyond a narrow pond; and the 130-yard 15th, a challenging, fascinating test, which between water, sand, cypress trees and some uneven terrain offers numerous ways to a disproportionally high score.

Despite modern equipment softening up even the hardest of courses, Spyglass still poses plenty of challenge to the world's best, with the aforementioned 446-yard 6th, the uphill 399-yard 8th and the 476-yard, dogleg-right 16th annually ranking among the toughest holes on the PGA Tour. Much of this continuing toughness comes from the one component equipment cannot substantially mitigate – the wind – but more than 40 years after its opening, the overall quality of Trent Jones's design should not be minimized. There are many who wish that more of his courses held this sort of flavour – but then how many sites offered these sorts of possibilities?

Taking play away from the coastal dunes, the 6th hole begins the long journey through the Del Monte Forest.

Riviera
Pacific Palisades, California

Set along the floor of Santa Monica canyon, in the once-sleepy Los Angeles suburb of Pacific Palisades, the Riviera Country Club has, since its 1926 inception, stood tall as southern California's most glamorous golfing address.

Riviera Country Club
Pacific Palisades, California

Designers: George Thomas and Billy Bell, 1926
Major events: US Open 1948; USPGA 1983, 1995; US Senior Open 1998

The Riviera Country Club has had a long and close association with Hollywood: since the early days of Douglas Fairbanks and Charlie Chaplin, actors and celebrities have held court at the club en masse.

To the public, however, its eminence derives from its being far and away the region's most prominent tournament venue. Riviera remains the only southern California course ever to host the US Open, in addition to two PGA championships, a US Senior Open and, on an annual basis, the PGA Tour's Los Angeles Open, now the Northern Trust Open. However, the biggest reason for Riviera's enduring fame is a much more fundamental one: it is, quite simply, one of the best-designed golf courses in the world.

GEORGE THOMAS'S MASTERPIECE

Riviera was built by Philadelphia-native George Thomas, an affluent Golden Age Renaissance man who never accepted payment for his work. Equally well known as a hybridizer of roses, a dog trainer, a fisherman and a writer, Thomas somehow found time to complete ten original golf-course designs after moving to Beverly Hills in 1919, including such additional area stalwarts as Bel-Air and the Los Angeles Country Club, and a full redesign/expansion of the 36-hole municipal facility at Griffith Park.

It was at Riviera that his skills were best displayed, for here was a compact, largely barren site that, except for a single narrow barranca, was nearly devoid of significant natural features. Yet on such unpromising land Thomas, with help from his construction man Billy Bell, created a strong,

CARD OF THE COURSE

HOLE	YARDS	PAR	HOLE	YARDS	PAR
1.	503	5	10.	315	4
2.	463	4	11.	564	5
3.	434	4	12.	479	4
4.	236	3	13.	459	4
5.	444	4	14.	176	3
6.	200	3	15.	487	4
7.	408	4	16.	166	3
8.	462	4	17.	590	5
9.	496	4	18.	475	4
OUT	**3,646**	**35**	**IN**	**3,711**	**36**
			TOTAL	**7,357**	**71**

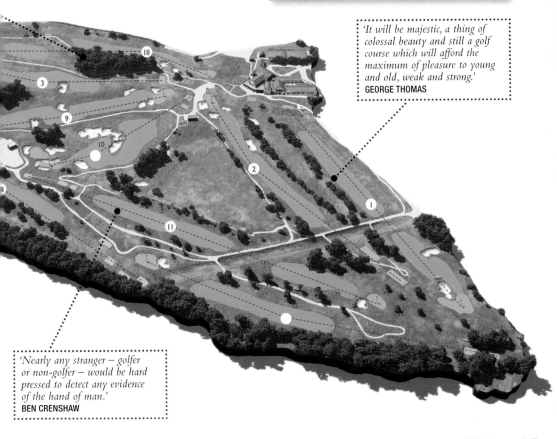

'It will be majestic, a thing of colossal beauty and still a golf course which will afford the maximum of pleasure to young and old, weak and strong.'
GEORGE THOMAS

'Nearly any stranger — golfer or non-golfer — would be hard pressed to detect any evidence of the hand of man.'
BEN CRENSHAW

yet beautifully varied layout – a golf course that has few peers in its number of architecturally significant holes. In addition, he managed to create a generously proportioned routing that still left more than enough room for modern lengthening – no small accomplishment on a tract measuring only 127 acres.

A CLASSIC START

Though primarily a flattish course, Riviera's 503-yard opener plays from a starkly elevated tee squeezed tightly against the grand Spanish-style clubhouse. It is a classic thinking-man's test: with a boomerang putting surface offering a wide variety of pin placements, players must effectively plan their shots from the green backwards. For a dead-straight hole with only two bunkers, it has few strategic equals.

After two stiff par fours running towards the property's lower reaches, the player encounters the 236-yard 4th, a hole once described by Ben Hogan as 'the greatest par three in America'. Generally played directly into the prevailing wind, the 4th offers two options: an all-carry route across a spectacular bunker, or a shot played right of the hazard, where a canted fairway helps the properly drawn ball reach the sloping putting surface.

PLAYING THE COURSE

The front nine's second par three is of perhaps even greater note, for the doughnut-like 6th features a large, two-tiered green famously perforated by a small bunker within the boundaries of the putting surface. The net effect is a green with four distinct quadrants – two high, two low – and all manner of fascinating pin positions, the most difficult of which is back-left. Long played at 165 yards, the modern addition of a 200-yard tournament tee makes for a particularly steep challenge indeed.

Often overlooked among Riviera's run of memorable holes is the 496-yard 9th, a par four with fairway bunkering perfectly positioned to test both the shorter and longer hitter. The approach is one of the club's most demanding, running slightly uphill to a narrow, steeply sloped green guarded front and left by notably deep bunkers. Perhaps the 9th is so underrated simply because it is followed by the 315-yard 10th, as strategically engrossing a short par four as exists in golf. Facing perhaps the most featureless expanse on the entire property – and a short one at that – George Thomas created a diminutive two-shotter played to a sloping, terribly narrow green, the rear two-thirds of which is tightly ringed by bunkers. From the tee the longer hitter is tempted to drive the green, but for most this is a sucker play because any ball coming up short or right leaves a nearly impossible pitch over sand, to a green falling steeply away. For most players, the smarter move is to lay up down the fairway's far-left side, leaving a much simpler pitch straight up the body of the putting surface. While equipment evolution has recently led most PGA Tour professionals to pull out the driver, for mere mortals this remains one of the game's grandest strategic tests.

The remainder of Riviera's back-nine par fours are far longer, with the 12th, 13th and 15th providing tournament tees measuring 479, 459 and 487 yards respectively – all played into the prevailing breeze. The 12th in particular does not require such length (the PGA Tour generally ignores its back tee), being a fine two-shotter played across the barranca to a green fronted right by a deep bunker and left by a grand sycamore tree. The 15th, on the other hand, doglegs around an imposing bunker, then requires a deft long-iron to a huge, deeply contoured green.

Riviera's compelling originality may not always translate well to television, for its finishers, though both varied and challenging, lack some of the visual flair apparent in many earlier holes. This does not prevent them from taking on a certain epic quality, however, particularly at the short, downhill 16th (its tiny, steep green surrounded by several splendid bunkers) and the memorable 475-yard 18th. This difficult two-shotter requires a pinpoint drive favouring the left side of a steeply elevated fairway, then a mid-iron to a green tucked into a large natural amphitheatre beneath the clubhouse.

DREADED KIKUYU

A further component in the Riviera equation is its sticky kikuyu grass – an ultra-hearty African strain originally brought in to stabilize the surrounding canyon walls against landslides. Today covering most of the layout, it makes for lush, carpet-like fairways but nightmarish rough, particularly affecting the delicate shots around the putting surface. It is, however, a seasonally sensitive grass, making Riviera, for the most part, a perceptibly tougher course in summer than during the cooler winter months.

The little pot-bunker at the centre of the green dictates that players must aim for the flag, not simply play to the middle.

Canada

Scottish fur traders are believed to have played golf in various
Canadian localities during the early years of the 19th century, and
other Scottish expatriates are known to have teed up in Montreal in
1826 and in Quebec City during the 1850s.

CANADA

22

29

8
11

10   23
16

20   30

Banff Springs
page 176

7
9
Vancouver

31

Victoria

6

The first club formed to play the modern game in North America was the Royal Montreal Golf Club[1], whose 1873 founding predates the earliest modern American golf club by 11 years. Unlike in America, however, the game did not expand with great rapidity; by the close of the 1870s only two additional clubs – in Quebec City and Brantford,

Ontario – had come into existence, and Royal Montreal remained, for several years, the game's de facto governing body.

There are now well over 1,700 courses in Canada. Though many thousands fewer than exist in the United States, this is really rather a sizeable number for a population of fewer than 30 million

Highlands Links
page 188
27

Ontario

2
5
14
18
26
19
24
25
Toronto
St George's
page 184

3
Quebec
Montreal
1
17

28

13

12
Brantford
Hamilton
page 180

4
15
21

Royal status was conferred on Colwood in 1931 following visits from the Prince of Wales.

and for a country with vast northern lands that are scarcely welcoming even to human population, never mind golf courses. Indeed, golf is today little seen in the Yukon and North-west Territories which, by themselves, are considerably larger than the great majority of the world's countries. Between them, they muster up only 72 holes of golf!

EARLY COURSES

Canada's lower provinces offered plenty of available people and land, however, and by the early 20th century course construction finally began to take off. One early designer of note was George Cumming, the 1905 Canadian Open champion and long-time professional at the Toronto Golf Club[2]. Another – rather more famous – designer was Willie Park Jnr, two-time Open champion and between 1905 and 1929 the builder of more than 20 Canadian courses including Quebec's Mount Bruno Golf and Country Club[3].

With its relative strategic sophistication, Park's work was in many ways ground-breaking, but in terms of a lasting legacy it was widely exceeded by that of his countryman Harry Colt, whose two brief visits to Canada yielded a pair of perennial favourites: Hamilton and Toronto. Also leaving a mark on the landscape was the legendary Donald Ross, who ventured up from America often enough to complete nearly a dozen projects, the most enduring of which are Ontario's Essex G and CC[4] and Rosedale[5], and Manitoba's St Charles Country Club[6], where Donald Ross and Alister MacKenzie each built nine holes. And then there was A. Vernon Macan, a native of Dublin, Ireland who emigrated to Canada in 1910 and practised architecture both there and in the American north-west. His list of Canadian courses numbers more than 20 and includes the very popular Royal Colwood[7], Shaughnessy[8] and Victoria[9], all located in British Columbia.

THE LEGACY OF STANLEY THOMPSON

The chief architect of Canada's prewar years was Stanley Thompson, the larger-than-life product of a fine golfing family. Over a 35-year design career, Thompson completed more than 145 projects, well over a hundred of these being

Opened in June 2012, Cabot Links is an exciting development on the Nova Scotia coast. This is the 415-yard 15th.

At Jasper National Park, golf is played against the magnificent backdrop of Canadian Rockies.

in Canada, and nearly half in his home province of Ontario. He began building courses in earnest in 1921, but his star would not fully rise until the opening of his 1926 design at Jasper National Park[10], a scenic and strategic wonder once cited as 'the best [course] I have ever seen' by the sometimes effusive Alister MacKenzie. Additional Thompson masterpieces included the spectacular Banff Springs, Cape Breton Highlands in Nova Scotia, St George's G and CC and Capilano[11], another splendidly scenic test situated in the foothills of West Vancouver, British Columbia.

A second tier of fine courses – although little known internationally – includes Westmount[12], Cataraqui[13], Oakdale[14] and Brantford[15], leaving Thompson, by a comfortable margin, as the major figure in Canadian golf design.

Stanley Thompson's influence did not end with his own courses, however. He also served as a mentor to several younger architects, among them Robert Trent Jones Snr, Geoffrey Cornish, Clinton 'Robbie' Robinson and Howard Watson. Robert Trent Jones built only four courses in Canada, highlighted by the Mount Kidd course

a period when several big-name American designers made brief, but important, northern appearances. In addition to Robert Trent Jones's cameos, Dick Wilson built an entirely new 27 holes for historic Royal Montreal[17] in 1959, while 1976 saw George and Tom Fazio add Ontario's National GC[18], and Jack Nicklaus design the frequent Canadian Open host Glen Abbey[19]. Nicklaus also returned in 1996 to build the best of four courses associated with the Chateau Whistler Resort[20], and has since added four more designs, three in British Columbia. Another foreign visitor, England's Donald Steel, followed in Harry Colt's footsteps by building one of the nation's best layouts during a brief 1990 visit – the minimalist Red Tail[21] in Ontario.

The modern era has also seen the rise of several important native designers, the first since Stanley Thompson to regularly build courses worthy of national – and even the occasional international – acclaim. High on this list is Rod Whitman, a former Pete Dye and Bill Coore associate whose skills are in evidence at Alberta's Blackhawk GC[22] and Wolf Creek Resort[23]. Past Robbie Robinson associate Doug Carrick has made a similar contemporary mark with nationally prominent courses such as the dune-covered Eagle's Nest[24], the Heathlands[25] course at Osprey Valley and Bigwin Island[26], all located in Ontario. Tom McBroom has also become popular, with Prince Edward Island's Links[27] at Crowbush Cove standing out among his more than 35 domestic works – a roster that includes a complete rebuild of Donald Ross's Algonquin Resort[28] course in New Brunswick, and the brand-new Tobiano[29] in Kamloops, British Columbia. Finally, Les Furber – a long-serving Trent Jones construction man – has completed more than 50 Canadian projects, the best received being the Predator Ridge[30] and Radium Resorts[31] both in British Columbia.

at Alberta's Kananaskis Country GC[16], while Geoffrey Cornish, a native of Winnipeg, lived in Massachusetts and added only five. But Robbie Robinson and Howard Watson contributed considerably to the nation's growing inventory of courses, designing more than 60 and 80 new layouts respectively, the vast majority in Ontario and, in Watson's case, Quebec.

POSTWAR ERA

Mirroring the United States, the immediate postwar years were a quiet time, leading into

Banff Springs
Banff, Alberta

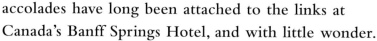

When a course is singled out from among its more than 30,000 worldwide competitors as being perhaps the most scenically beautiful, that is one very grand – and alluring – statement indeed. Such accolades have long been attached to the links at Canada's Banff Springs Hotel, and with little wonder.

**Banff Springs Golf Course
(Thompson course)**
Banff, Alberta

Designer: Stanley Thompson, 1929

Set in a spectacular corner of the Canadian Rockies, flanked by the Bow and Spray rivers and surrounded by towering peaks and thick pine forests, the Banff Springs layout surely has to qualify as one of the world's prettiest places, golf-related or otherwise. To such a spot tourists flowed early and often, with the Rocky Mountain National Park established in 1887, the first Banff Springs Hotel opening a year later and the present hotel – a massive limestone edifice and one of the world's most recognizable hostelries – taking in its first visitors in 1914.

EARLY HISTORY

Golf at Banff Springs dates to a rudimentary nine holes built in 1911, followed by a short-lived Donald Ross 18-hole course begun in 1917 but not completed until the early 1920s. Little-recorded today, the Ross layout met its demise when, in 1926, up-and-coming Canadian architect Stanley Thompson opened a highly praised course at nearby Jasper National Park. This prompted Banff Springs's owners, the Canadian Pacific Railway, quickly to hire Thompson to build them something comparable.

A large, flamboyant man with a similarly colourful design style, Thompson was a highly strategic architect with a knack for integrating his flashy bunkering into the natural flow of the landscape. This particular landscape, however, proved a difficult one on which to work, and after felling thousands of trees and dynamiting countless

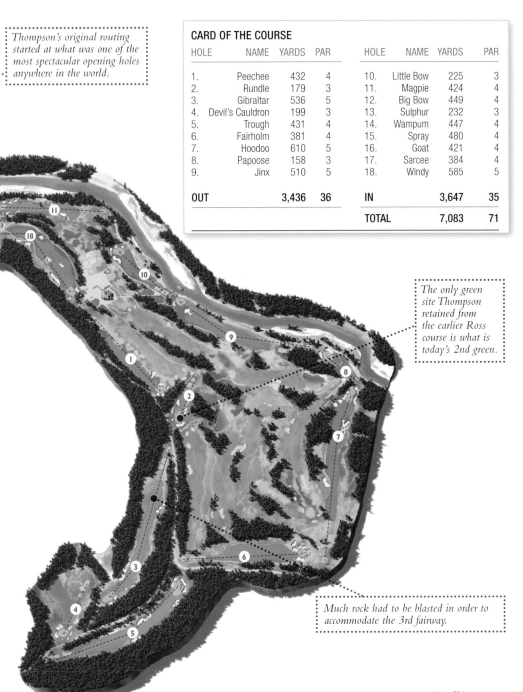

CARD OF THE COURSE

HOLE	NAME	YARDS	PAR	HOLE	NAME	YARDS	PAR
1.	Peechee	432	4	10.	Little Bow	225	3
2.	Rundle	179	3	11.	Magpie	424	4
3.	Gibraltar	536	5	12.	Big Bow	449	4
4.	Devil's Cauldron	199	3	13.	Sulphur	232	3
5.	Trough	431	4	14.	Wampum	447	4
6.	Fairholm	381	4	15.	Spray	480	4
7.	Hoodoo	610	5	16.	Goat	421	4
8.	Papoose	158	3	17.	Sarcee	384	4
9.	Jinx	510	5	18.	Windy	585	5
OUT		**3,436**	**36**	**IN**		**3,647**	**35**
				TOTAL		**7,083**	**71**

The only green site Thompson retained from the earlier Ross course is what is today's 2nd green.

Much rock had to be blasted in order to accommodate the 3rd fairway.

Six holes, from the 9th to the 14th, benefit from the company of the Bow River.

tons of rock, the man who would ultimately be viewed as Canada's greatest-ever designer found himself making history with the world's first $1 million golf course. The results, happily, were hardly out of line with the hefty price.

A MODERN RESEQUENCING

It is worth noting that while nearly all of Thompson's design – though lengthened – remains either intact or restored, the 1989 addition of nine new holes (with an associated clubhouse situated more than a mile from the hotel) led to a complete resequencing of the original 18. Lost in this process was the opportunity to walk just a few feet from the main house to the putting green and practice area and, more importantly, to start play at what is now the 15th hole. There an elevated tee shot across the rushing waters of the Spray, aimed

directly towards the slopes of Mount Rundle, was among the most dazzling openings in all of golf.

If nothing else, the present configuration of the course introduces one of the game's most famous holes earlier – the 199-yard Devil's Cauldron 4th (formerly the 8th) – which is as scenically beautiful a test as any golfer might ever hope to encounter. Playing from an elevated tee, it requires a mid-iron carried across a glacial pond to a green built against the base of Mount Rundle, whose rock and pine-covered face towers almost dizzyingly above it. The green itself is fairly small and flanked by six bunkers, but it is also somewhat concave and surrounded by punchbowl-like terrain that draws marginal shots towards the centre. The challenge, really, is to summon forth even that marginal shot in the face of this once-in-a-lifetime setting.

RIVERSIDE HOLES

Having begun along the base of Mount Rundle for the first five holes, play soon progresses northwards across the valley floor, with the shortish 6th and very long 7th (a genuine three-shotter for all but the longest of hitters) leading to the banks of the Bow, and a stretch of seven attractive waterside holes. In some cases the river is merely a scenic distraction, loosely paralleling play, while in others it or one of its smaller spurs is brought directly into the action. An example of the latter is the gorgeous 158-yard 8th, little more than a pitch in the 1-mile high altitude, but one played to a sloping green fronted by water and backed by sand. Following the majestic 510-yard 9th, the 225-yard 10th also requires a water carry and, the Devil's Cauldron not withstanding, is surely the most testing of Banff's par threes.

Following the heavily bunkered 11th, the 449-yard 12th is a stunning two-shotter whose wide fairway progressively narrows to a triangular-shaped green guarded left by sand and right by the immediately adjacent river. The 232-yard 13th and 447-yard 14th are of similar (if slightly dryer) stuff. It is well worth reflecting at this stage that these were Thompson's final holes before the complete resequencing that took place in 1989, with the 14th in particular – highlighted by its inspiring view across the treetops to the soaring frontage of the hotel – seeming oddly out of place at this juncture.

From here the golfer plays the 480-yard 15th (from the former 1st tee), then returns to the slopes of Mount Rundle for a three-hole dash, which concludes at the 585-yard 18th. This is a solid downwind par five made interesting by a deep dead-centre bunker some 125 yards in front of the green.

GETTING ADJUSTED

Though filled with challenging, beautifully conceived holes, the biggest test at Banff Springs is probably a mental one, because the massive scale of Thompson's bunkering can be deceiving to the inexperienced eye – and that is before considering the roughly 10 per cent greater carry created by the high mountain altitude. Furthermore, it takes a remarkable degree of focus not to be distracted by the jaw-dropping surroundings, and visitors must surely be forgiven for missing many of the course's subtleties during their first or second go-rounds.

It is difficult to conceive of a layout of greater all-round beauty. If somehow Banff Springs is not the world's most scenic, it surely must be its prettiest genuinely great golf course, which in itself is not a bad platform to occupy.

One of the most photographed holes in the world, the 4th, Devil's Cauldron, rarely fails to tighten the golfer's knuckles.

Hamilton
Ancaster, Ontario

Harry Colt's visit to the greater Toronto area in 1914 had a profound effect – directly and indirectly – on Canada's golf scene. Having designed the charming Toronto GC, he then laid out the brawny Hamilton Golf and Country Club at Ancaster. Although the styles may have been similar, Hamilton's scale is larger than Toronto GC, both in terms of the raw property and the architectural features that would match it.

Hamilton Golf and Country Club
Ancaster, Ontario

Designer: Harry Colt, 1916
Major events: Canadian Open 1919, 1930, 2003, 2006, 2012

Colt's indirect influence on Canadian golf-course architecture was rather fortuitous. Hamilton's long-time professional Nichol Thompson (who retired in 1945 after 37 years of service) played a key role in not only shaping Hamilton but also Canadian golf in general. In association with Toronto GC's professional George Cumming, the two would both as a duo and in consultation with Nichol's younger brother, Stanley, design courses throughout the greater Toronto area. These served as a launch pad for young Stanley Thompson, who went on to become a full-time designer – and Canada's most revered. Although their styles differed, it is clear that Colt's early architecture at Toronto and Hamilton proved the foundation and

inspiration for many of the clubs the trio would later go on to create.

COURSE CHANGES

Ancaster as the course is called (named after the town that borders the industrial centre of Hamilton) opened in 1916 in its third location since the club's founding in 1894. Colt's work was carried out by the club's John Sutherland, and he

CARD OF THE COURSE

HOLE	YARDS	PAR	HOLE	YARDS	PAR
1.	404	4	10.	412	4
2.	431	4	11.	481	4
3.	408	4	12.	383	4
4.	532	5	13.	234	3
5.	318	4	14.	443	4
6.	224	3	15.	415	4
7.	411	4	16.	185	3
8.	210	3	17.	548	5
9.	438	4	18.	442	4
OUT	3,376	35	IN	3,543	35
			TOTAL	6,919	70

never returned to the course, although his design partner Charles Alison visited in 1920. Alison's suggestions centred on the desire to make the bunkers more penal. The most drastic change was the rebuilding of the par-three 13th, which Alison felt was too severe. These adaptations formed the final touches of the Colt–Alison team at Ancaster and stood until 1974, when the addition of the third nine caused further alterations to the course. With the expansion nine claiming the 15th green and reorienting the 16th tee, the course found its current incarnation.

Ancaster's transformations through the years have also included changes from bunkering – some deserted, others altered – to tree planting (followed by removal) and lastly amendments to several greens. Despite these, the unifying theme at Ancaster is Colt's exemplar routing through this property with its great terrain and massive scale. He placed tees and greens at the high points and required the golfer to play down and back out of the valleys. Thankfully, the stream that trickled through the property provided a wide ground for golf. Given the stress Colt placed on one-shotters, it is not surprising that he created par threes when some of the most dramatic (but also difficult) land came to be used. A sense of this can be found at the 8th. Renowned for his heathland designs, Colt must have marvelled at the drama that the rolling land allowed.

COLT'S LEGACY

Nowhere are Colt's traits more evident than on the 408-yard 3rd, which plays dramatically downhill to a fairway bisected by the stream that he routed cleverly around and over on numerous holes. When planning the tee shot, the player must try to leave a comfortable distance to approach the uphill green, which is one of the toughest on the course. Shallow and quick, the front-left pin is not to be tussled with, but rather a well-played shot to the centre of the green is always prudent.

Once again taking advantage of the wonderful natural terrain at the 318-yard 5th, Colt created a masterful, short par four. Arguably the most difficult hole to design to this high level, it is as

delightful today as it was on opening day. With the green perched on a hillock and the fairway flowing left to right, the approach is difficult, whether with a daring driver or a delicate short-iron. Colt did leave room in front to run the ball into the green, but with the slope of the fronting fairway it does require an exacting drive. Perhaps two of the most difficult recoveries faced at Ancaster are revealed to golfers who miss either right or long and have to contend with the steep slope of the hill and small putting surface as a target.

DRAMATIC PAR THREES

After the strong set of opening holes, Colt's prowess with par threes is amply displayed at the 6th and the 8th. The former plays to a brutish 224 yards and, although it is only slightly uphill, the hole manages to seem longer. Colt cleverly placed two bunkers into the hillside short of the green, to create the illusion that they were flush against the front of the green. However, this was simply an optical trick, because the bunkers are well short and rarely come into play. Colt further used some of the most dramatic terrain for the 8th, on which the player is faced with a do-or-die par three, measuring 210 yards. Playing from ridge to ridge, bisected by the river valley, it manages to produce one of Ancaster's prettiest yet also most difficult shots.

On making the turn, Colt created a nifty three-hole loop to begin the back nine. Each of the trio holes crosses the stream and plays within the broader loop of the front nine, before the 12th turns east and begins to open up the rest of the back nine. This hole is one of the highlights. Playing to a modest 383 yards, the gentle hole plays back uphill into a benched green, set into the hillside. With trees flanking both sides of the fairway, the player must stay alert and accurate to prevent a stroke slipping away.

The 3rd playing through a valley illustrates the broad canvas provided to Harry Colt for his design.

Alison's redesigned 13th blends seamlessly into the overall design, although the 415-yard 15th and 185-yard 16th bore the greatest brunt of the changes to Colt's routing, and sadly the course is not better for them.

A MEMORABLE ENDING

Hamilton has a strong finish with the 548-yard 17th followed by the 442-yard 18th – one of the great closers in Canada, where the meandering stream's central role at Ancaster reaches its peak. Quite literally snaking across the fairway at the 300-yard mark, only the longest hitters can reach it from the tee. However, its presence causes many golfers to ease off, which can lead to a ball that fails to funnel to the ideal spot and forces a long and arduous uphill second shot.

Hamilton's stately clubhouse (which was built 13 years after the golf course opened) looms large as the backdrop of the closing green complex, and the uphill nature results in many shots left short. It was here at the 2003 Canadian Open that Bob Tway defeated Brad Faxon, with a bogey from the green-side bunker.

High drama at the last has cemented Ancaster's role in professional golf's history, but it was Harry Colt's brilliant routing over wonderful terrain that makes the course worthy of study to this day.

St George's
Etobicoke, Ontario

Laid out by Stanley Thompson in 1929, St George's original charge was to provide golf facilities for the Royal York – the stately downtown hotel whose name it bore. By 1946, the arrangement with the hotel had come to an end and henceforth the club became St George's Golf and Country Club.

St George's Golf and Country Club
Etobicoke, Ontario

Designers: Stanley Thompson, 1929 and Robbie Robinson, 1966
Major events: Canadian Open 1949, 1960, 1968, 2010

'This hole symbolizes the appeal of the two-shot holes at St. George's. There is plenty of room off the tee. The green complex has four uniquely shaped bunkers, the type that only Thompson built and that characterize his courses.' **RAN MORRISSETT**

Stanley Thompson's flamboyant style in life mimicked the grandiose designs that made him famous. What St George's lacked in natural beauty Thompson made up for with a wonderful layout. Saving the most severe points for dramatic par threes, he would both attack and retreat within the routing, providing enormous diversity. Using his trademark bunkering – which rivalled only

CARD OF THE COURSE

HOLE	YARDS	PAR	HOLE	YARDS	PAR
1.	370	4	10.	377	4
2.	466	4	11.	528	5
3.	198	3	12.	399	4
4.	474	5	13.	213	3
5.	432	4	14.	466	4
6.	201	3	15.	570	5
7.	446	4	16.	203	3
8.	223	3	17.	470	4
9.	538	5	18.	451	4
OUT	**3,348**	**35**	**IN**	**3,677**	**36**
			TOTAL	**7,025**	**71**

Thompson died in 1953 and so his right-hand man Robbie Robinson handled the changes, which ranged from slight modifications to rather significant alterations such as a complete rebuilding of the par-three 3rd, which remains bemusing to this day.

In 2002 architect Ian Andrew, of Carrick Design, was employed to restore the bunker style of Thompson, which had been lost through many years of maintenance and change, and he remarked:

'St George's is a testament to Thompson's ability to create bold enough bunkering to draw your attention, yet artistic enough to still blend seamlessly into the surrounding landscape.'

In the 2010 Canadian Open, Swede, Carl Pettersson, shot a 60 in the third round to set up an eventual victory.

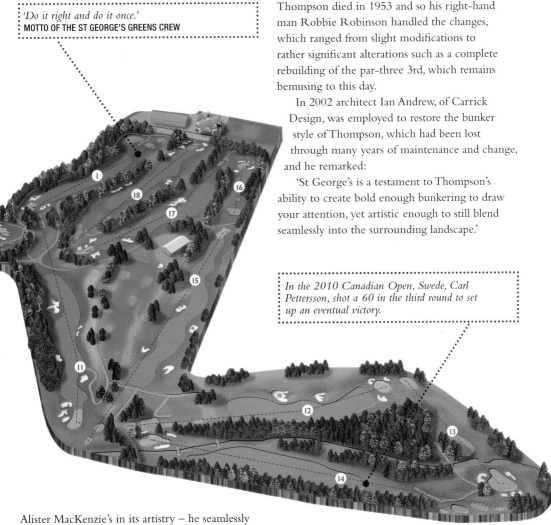

Alister MacKenzie's in its artistry – he seamlessly fitted St George's hazards within the big scale of the property.

LATER COURSE ALTERATIONS

Although St George's played host to its first of four Canadian Opens in 1949, the course was lengthened only for the tournament, held in 1968.

CLUBHOUSE POSITION DILEMMA

Beginning its journey on the east side of Islington Avenue, the course opens gently with a nearly perfect welcome to the round. From the elevated 1st tee play is down to a slender fairway, before

While the 2nd hole may be tough and demanding it is also undeniably attractive.

climbing again to the well-protected green site. Thompson, however, did not generally subscribe to such a 'gentle handshake' to open the round. He always believed that the current 1st would be the closing par four and that golf would begin on the current, difficult, 466-yard 2nd, which is situated beside an ideal area for a clubhouse. In the end the clubhouse was not built there but over the road, away from the course. The actual reason for the unorthodox separation of the clubhouse and course is not known for certain, but the theory advanced by the club is that bar facilities could be included if the clubhouse was positioned on the west side of Islington Avenue, and not if it were to be set amid the course itself on the east side of the road, where the drinking laws were different.

Although the 1966 changes to the 198-yard 3rd are out of character with the rest of the course, Robinson's relocation of the 4th green into the hillside added length to both the 474-yard 4th and 432-yard 5th. Here, though, Thompson's routing of

the course through the valleys is what really stands out, and where they were most severe he crossed them, as on the delicious par-three 6th.

The 446-yard 7th seemingly plays longer than the 466-yard 2nd, because of its steady rise from tee to green. Thompson swings golfers left with a large bunker that dominates the right side of the fairway, then forces them back-right with a large bunker short-left. This clever approach gives the feeling of a double-dogleg in what is a straight corridor. Favouring the more aggressive line on both the drive and approach can shorten the hole significantly, while allowing the golfer to approach from the preferred angle. Though Thompson created ample fairway on the left side of the 7th, the approach shot is then over a difficult bunker complex to a green that slopes to the front and right. Contours of the green demand special attention, and many golfers have surely wished to have been 10 yards shorter with their chipping club than face a long putt on this beguiling green.

Using 'nature as his guide' as Thompson was prone to say, the golfer can smile at the 223-yard 8th. With the green nestled behind a hillside, the majority of the putting surface is hidden, yet Thompson was smart in his use of the natural landform. A large bunker on the left side, which appears to the eye as flush against the green, is actually well short and a ball that manages to carry it continues down the hill and onto the receptive green. In following the flows of the land, Thompson managed to inject some controversy, while allowing for a surprisingly playable hole.

HANDSOME, UNDULATING COURSE

Thompson's stretch of golf from the 10th to the 12th provides a striking example of his use of the topography. Although at 377 yards the 10th is a relatively short par four that looks fairly flat from the tee, this visual trick is revealed by a valley that collects most drives, leaving a blind, short-iron approach. Finding a level stance can only be secured by laying well back of the valley, but few take this longer route. From the 11th tee, the golfer plunges back down into the valley, and the elevation allows the stronger golfer a chance at birdie if the well-staggered bunkers can be avoided.

Climbing out of the valley at the 399-yard 12th, the golfer faces the most dramatic bunker complex on the course, which lures tee shots just left of this fairway. An abrupt 12-foot rise to the table-top green, which sits on a hillock, leaves ticklish approaches to a front hole location.

Playing steadily downhill, the 466-yard 14th requires a strong drive to catch the sloping fairway and gain advantage of the topography. Level lies can be a great reward, because the approach is what garners this hole's fame. Hugging the right side of the area and bisecting the hole is a stream,

which then meanders in front and guards the left greenside. With three bunkers guarding the hillside green, disaster looms for a weaker shot. Relatively subdued, the putting surface is a welcome respite.

Stern back-to-back par fours – the 470-yard 17th and 451-yard 18th – make nursing a good score down the final stretch a tall order. Indeed, St George's as it stands today may be Thompson's toughest test, but with great land and restored bunkers it also reflects his great style. Interestingly, on its opening, the course was not considered among Thompson's more picturesque ones – these being Banff Springs, Capilano, Highlands Links and Jasper Park. Perhaps the greatest testament to Thompson as a designer is that as St George's has matured it has come to be considered an equal to his other famous designs.

A stream crossing the fairway bunkers dictates the outcome on the later stages of the 14th hole.

Highlands Links
Ingonish Beach, Nova Scotia

During the Great Depression in the early 1930s, Canada suffered economic hardship. Therefore the federal government, wanting to capitalize on the success of Banff Springs and Jasper Park in attracting visitors, sought to establish a great golf course on the eastern tip of Canada. Thus Highlands Links was born.

Highlands Links
Ingonish Beach, Nova Scotia

Designer: Stanley Thompson, 1941

as he walked the land and studied the aerial photographs, Thompson became keen to do an 18-hole routing. When the nine holes then cost $12,500 below the $70,000 budget, Thompson convinced the authorities to extend the golf course. Of the original nine, it would use holes

Cape Breton Highlands Links (the name has since been shortened to Highlands Links) was created on a spit of land called Middle Head Peninsula. This is barely wide enough to accommodate the parallel opening and closing holes, because it juts into the Atlantic. Famous Canadian architect Stanley Thompson first came to the site on Cape Breton Island, Nova Scotia, in 1937. Even though he had already designed courses on several outstanding sites, such as at Banff and Jasper, Thompson still found the setting of Cape Breton to be spectacular.

Originally, the government's commission was to create a nine-hole course. However,

'I introduced the crew to "chunking" where we excavate the fescue bank in large chunks and then puzzle it back together to create all the noses and lost lines where the bunker is filled in.'
ARCHITECT IAN ANDREW ON RESTORATION WORK ON THE 17TH HOLE.

CARD OF THE COURSE

HOLE	NAME	YARDS	PAR		HOLE	NAME	YARDS	PAR
1.	Ben Franey	405	4		10.	Cuddy's Lugs	145	3
2.	Tam O'Shanter	447	4		11.	Bonnie Burn	512	5
3.	Lochan	160	3		12.	Cleugh	240	3
4.	Heich O'Fash	324	4		13.	Laird	435	4
5.	Canny Slap	164	3		14.	Haugh	398	4
6.	Mucklemouth Meg	537	5		15.	Tattie Bogle	540	5
7.	Killiecrankie	570	5		16.	Sair Fecht	460	5
8.	Caber's Toss	319	4		17.	Dowie Den	190	3
9.	Corbie's Nest	336	4		18.	Hame Noo	410	4
OUT		**3,262**	**36**		**IN**		**3,330**	**36**
					TOTAL		**6,592**	**72**

'Every now and then I get a mean streak and like to fool the boys a little. But, I never hide any danger. It's all out there for the golfer to see and study.'
STANLEY THOMPSON

'The bunkers at Cape Breton play "bigger" than their actual size, thanks to some clever mounding by Thompson.'
RAN MORRISSETT

1 to 4 and 14 to 18. His new routing was both on a coastal stretch, which dominate holes 1 to 6, and on some 'mountainous' terrain, which begins at the 7th. Although pressure was put on Thompson to extend the holes farther up the coast, beyond the 6th, he remained certain that the best golf was offered by turning west into the hills and up the Clyburn Valley. Having won over his patrons, it is little surprise that the 7th, named Killiecrankie, is arguably Canada's best par five. To access the extra land up the valley, several local residents had their land expropriated, something Thompson paid tribute to in his naming of the 13th hole Laird after these displaced residents.

MANUAL LABOUR

Because the government undertook the Highlands Links project not only to create a future draw for tourism but also to generate work for the locals, it took measures to ensure the latter requirement was met. Only two pieces of excavation equipment were permitted on site, and their use was restricted to one day a week. Thus the construction crew swelled to as many as 180 at a given time and provided 300–400 jobs for local labourers. Given the severity of the terrain and the presence of rocks, a great deal of work was done by hand.

Such attention to detail resulted in a golf course with some fine architectural points,

The 15th hole combines majestic vistas with the wonderful land that makes the course so unique.

including great fairway contours and a marvellous set of greens. These are an undulating set that (with the exception of a repair to the 13th) mercifully have not been tampered with through the years. Thompson achieved many of the unruly contours at Highlands Links by burying piles of rocks in the fairway, thereby creating humps and bumps reminiscent of the Scottish courses that he loved.

PLAYING THE CONTOURS

Such uneven terrain is very much in evidence on the stern uphill 1st, with its lumpy fairway. However, the task facing the golfer gets harder at the 447-yard 2nd. Widely hailed as one of the finest bunkerless par fours in golf. Its heaving fairway doglegs right. As the corner is rounded the dramatic vista of the Atlantic as the backdrop to the tremendous 2nd green is revealed.

From here the golfer plays north along the coast for the next four holes. Diversity is the key – the 3rd and 6th greens are at sea level and their surrounds are comparatively flat. In contrast to the well-defended pulpit 4th green, the 5th green plays bigger than it actually is as its sides and back help gather approach shots.

Highlands Links was a walking-only course until 1997 and every serious golfer still delights in the walk today. As they cross the bridge over the Clyburn river – often with fishermen below – they sense the unique connection with nature that Thompson felt at this site some 80 years earlier. On crossing the bridge, the oceanside is left for the mountains and the 7th tee. With its wonderfully undulating ground, this 570-yard par five feels a worthy foil to the ocean. Its land formations flow from the left, then the right, so the player must thread a drive into the narrow chute. From the landing area, the hole rises steadily to the wild green that caps this hole.

On finishing the 12th, the golfer experiences something that is rarely found on a golf course – something that Thompson believed to be a key component to the course. A walking path of nearly 500 yards hugs tightly to the river bank and is barely wide enough for playing partners to walk side by side. The walk's serenity appropriately embodies the entire golf experience.

A strong drive is required at the 13th to find the fairway, which cants heavily from right to left and allows two distinct levels of play. The higher, right side affords more short grass and the clearer angle, while the lower left allows the use of slope as a springboard and shortens the hole significantly. Thompson carefully shaped the fairway leading into the green with a generous slope to feed the ball in.

THE CLOSING HOLES

Marking the turn for home is another set of back-to-back par fives. Again, Thompson uses the natural slope to dare the stronger player to hug the tree line left and carry the hillock to be rewarded with a level lie and a chance to get home in two on the 540-yard 15th. Nevertheless, most drives find the fairway right and are forced to lay up over the hill to a heavily bunkered landing area. On coming up over the rise, the vista is once again extraordinary, with the aptly named Whale Island in the background and the church steeple in the foreground. This culmination at the 15th makes it easy to see why Thompson labelled Highlands his 'mountains and oceans course'.

One of Highlands Links's great attributes relative to Thompson's other works is highlighted at the last two holes, namely that the greens are still largely as he designed them. The undulations found in these 17th and 18th putting surfaces display Thompson's flair for green construction, and they make for a fitting finish to the course.

Central America and the Atlantic islands

Apart from Mexico and Costa Rica, most of Central America remains on a colonial-era golf footing, with the game enjoying only small pockets of popularity, usually in areas populated by foreign nationals or the odd affluent native. In the islands the golfing emphasis is on resort golf.

Golf's first recorded appearance in Mexico came in 1897. The game's initial popularity there, however, was limited to a handful of courses frequented by British or American businessmen, and the occasional local. This changed only after the Second World War when Percy Clifford, a Briton born and raised in Mexico, enlisted the help of both the government and American designer Lawrence Hughes in building the Club de Golf Mexico[1] (twice a World Cup host). This was easily the nation's first truly prominent facility. Clifford and Hughes went on to enjoy prolific design careers in Mexico, with Clifford actually building nearly half of the roughly 80 layouts that dotted the country c.1980.

A handful of courses (notably Clifford's Vallescondido[2]) vied with the Club de Golf Mexico for period superiority, but even these are today largely overshadowed by a resort boom that began in the long-established Acapulco, Mazatlán and Cancun,

before spreading to a variety of locations, mostly along the Pacific coast. With frequent pushes from a tourism-friendly government, Puerto Vallarta, Manzanillo, Ixtapa and even the less-glamorous Tijuana/Ensenada region near the American border now offer golfing destinations on par with many of the finest resorts in the hemisphere, often featuring courses built by American designers such as Robert Trent Jones Jnr, Jack Nicklaus and Robert von Hagge. The unquestioned centre of Mexican resort golf, however, is the Los Cabos/ Cabo San Lucas area at the southern tip of Baja California, where the Nicklaus name is king, and seaside/desert golf of a very high calibre abounds.

Costa Rica is a growing American tourism/ retirement destination, and a country in which Jack Nicklaus, Robert von Hagge and Arnold Palmer have all designed golf courses for the mass market. Palmer's resort course at Papagayo explores a dense tropical forest yet enjoys great ocean views.

TYPICAL ISLANDS COURSES

Golf in the Atlantic Islands has, for the most part, always been resort-based, initially on a small scale in British-controlled Bermuda and the Bahamas, then, during the 1960s and '70s, in Puerto Rico, Jamaica and the Dominican Republic. Today the game has grabbed a strong foothold – usually in association with one luxury resort or another – on almost every island large enough to hold it, from New Providence to Aruba.

Bermuda was home to the region's first great layout, Mid Ocean, and today mixes the old with the new. Robert Trent Jones Snr's Port Royal[3] (1970) and Roger Rulewich's Tucker's Point[4] – a 2003 rebuild of the old Castle Harbour Golf Course – are among the island's best.

In the Bahamas, early golf was played primarily by British expatriates around Nassau, but today the game has reached most of the country's major islands. On Great Abaco there is Dick Wilson's Treasure Cay GC[5], while Grand Bahama is highlighted by 36 holes at the Lucaya resort in the form of Dick Wilson's Lucayan course[6] (which dates from 1962) and by Robert Trent Jones Jnr's Reef course[7], an addition in 2000. Great Exuma offers Greg Norman's spectacular design at the Four Seasons Emerald Bay[8], where six holes occupy a narrow oceanfront peninsula, while New Providence golf includes the Bahamas' oldest course – the much-altered Cable Beach GC[9] – as well as Dick Wilson's once-prominent 1960 design

Generally regarded as 'the first course of genuine character' in the Caribbean, Tryall was designed by Ralph Plummer.

at Lyford Cay and Tom Weiskopf's remodel of an early Wilson work on Paradise Island.

OTHER PRE-EMINENT COURSES

For a former British colony, Jamaica came to golf relatively slowly and, though a handful of prewar layouts still exist, its best courses are of a decidedly newer vintage, particularly those clustered along the north shore, around Montego Bay. The oldest of the bunch, the Tryall GC[10], is from 1958 and, although altered a bit in recent years, remains among the elite of the Caribbean. Close on its heels came Robert Trent Jones Snr's 1961 design at Half-Moon Bay, which today is part of a 54-hole Rose Hall[11] resort facility that includes a pair of newer Robert von Hagge designs – Cinnamon Hill and the spectacular White Witch.

The Dominican Republic became a sudden fashionable golfing destination in 1971 with the debut of Pete Dye's spectacular Casa de Campo, and this La Romana resort has since added two more Dye courses to go with yet another of his highly rated creations, the nearby La

Although Mahogany Run on St Thomas is hardly a great course, its cliff-top sequence of holes, the Devil's Triangle, is fun.

Romana Country Club[12]. The Dye name carries considerable weight in these parts still, because Pete's son P.B. has built several Dominican courses, including an exciting coastal course at the Punta Cana resort, a popular destination at the island's eastern tip. An earlier Robert Trent Jones presence can still be felt here as well, with his work at Playa Grande[13] and the Santo Domingo CC[14] generally rating among the island's best.

The American territory of Puerto Rico was an early player in regional golf development and today features four 36-hole resorts of distinction: Dorado Beach[15] (East and West Courses by Robert Trent Jones), Cerromar[16] (North and South Courses also by Robert Trent Jones), Rio Mar[17] (Ocean Course by George Fazio, River by Greg Norman) and Palmas del Mar [18](Palm Course by Gary Player, Flamboyan by Rees Jones). Also noteworthy is the El Conquistador resort[19], once a wildly distinctive Robert von Hagge creation since entirely renovated by Arthur Hills.

SMALLER ISLAND ATTRACTIONS

Several courses of merit dot smaller islands, led by Robert Trent Jones Snr's well-known Carambola GC[20] (née Fountain Valley) on St Croix and George and Tom Fazio's Mahogany Run GC[21] on St Thomas, a shortish layout featuring some spectacular cliff-top terrain.

Anguilla offers Greg Norman's Temenos GC[22], while Robert Trent Jones Jnr left his mark at three note-worthy facilities: the Four Seasons resort in Nevis[23], Aruba's windswept Tierra del Sol[24] and Barbados's stylish Royal Westmoreland[25]. Also in Barbados is a pair of Tom Fazio designs at the Sandy Lane resort[26] – the Country Club and Green Monkey Courses. And finally, the southern island of Tobago features the Mount Irvine Bay Hotel GC[27], a 1969 design by John Harris, the former Royal Navy commander who built a number of distinctive 1960s and '70s courses in the tropics.

Robert Trent Jones created some uncompromising golf courses, but also the user-friendly layout of Four Seasons in Nevis.

Casa de Campo
La Romana, Dominican Republic

Widely rated among the world's finest courses immediately upon its opening in 1971, Pete Dye's Casa de Campo certainly succeeded in making the Dominican Republic an international golfing destination of note in the Caribbean.

Casa de Campo (Teeth of the Dog)
La Romana, Dominican Republic

Designer: Pete Dye, 1971

Probably more than any high-profile designer of the postwar era, Pete Dye has long had a reputation for, to borrow from Ben Hogan, finding his golf courses 'in the dirt'. He has always created courses the old-fashioned way by walking his properties, selecting his routing, then working out his design concepts on the ground, shaping them as he goes.

WORKING WITH THE LAND

Such a painstaking, traditional approach has served Dye well over the course of his six-decade career, but surely nowhere more so than at Casa de Campo, on the south-east coast of the Dominican Republic. Known alternatively as 'Cajuiles' (the name of a local cashew tree) or 'Teeth of the Dog' (after the jagged-edged coral that inhabits the property), Casa de Campo began life as a way for the Gulf and Western Corporation to invest its local sugar production profits into Dominican tourist development. As such, the decision was made to

build the sort of golf course that would attract attention in the faraway American markets so vital to the Caribbean winter trade. With the company owning 400,000 acres, Dye had a marvellous selection of coastal sites to choose from, though in the end he still managed to exceed the property boundaries, necessitating the last-minute purchase of several adjoining tracts.

Because state-of-the-art earthmoving equipment was scarce in the Dominican Republic in 1971, Dye had to put together a workforce of locals to reshape the property by hand. Initially this involved clearing dense underbrush with machetes, though more challenging tasks included carting

away hundreds of boulders and blasting – with hand tools, not dynamite – the coral patches that dotted the coastal expanse. The disintegrated coral was often laid, piece by piece, into the small walls that line select bunkers and, in perhaps the most labour-intensive construction move on record, several fairways were actually hand planted, blade by painstaking blade. As Dye later rather understatedly wrote: 'The opportunity to carve out Teeth of the Dog was a once-in-a-lifetime experience.'

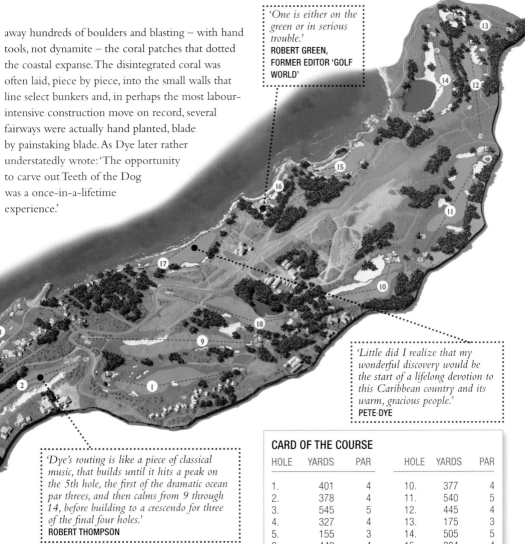

> '*One is either on the green or in serious trouble.*'
> **ROBERT GREEN, FORMER EDITOR 'GOLF WORLD'**

> '*Little did I realize that my wonderful discovery would be the start of a lifelong devotion to this Caribbean country and its warm, gracious people.*'
> **PETE·DYE**

> '*Dye's routing is like a piece of classical music, that builds until it hits a peak on the 5th hole, the first of the dramatic ocean par threes, and then calms from 9 through 14, before building to a crescendo for three of the final four holes.*'
> **ROBERT THOMPSON**

SEVEN OCEANFRONT HOLES

Casa de Campo includes nearly 3 miles of ocean frontage, which allowed a total of seven holes (four on the front, three on the back) to be built directly on the water. The clubhouse, however, lies inland, necessitating an opening run of four dry

CARD OF THE COURSE

HOLE	YARDS	PAR	HOLE	YARDS	PAR
1.	401	4	10.	377	4
2.	378	4	11.	540	5
3.	545	5	12.	445	4
4.	327	4	13.	175	3
5.	155	3	14.	505	5
6.	449	4	15.	384	4
7.	225	3	16.	185	3
8.	417	4	17.	435	4
9.	505	5	18.	440	4
OUT	**3,402**	**36**	**IN**	**3,486**	**36**
			TOTAL	**6,888**	**72**

How the ocean-side holes at Teeth of the Dog play depends entirely on the wind, its speed and direction. This is the 7th hole.

holes of varied lengths, a quartet brought to life by several vast waste bunkers, a touch of replication – the 4th, for example, is loosely based on the 3rd at Pinehurst No 2 – and their routing into the prevailing east wind.

The course takes on an epic quality, however, immediately on reaching the water, with the 155-yard 5th setting the tone. Here a narrow, almost crescent-shaped green sits on a rocky outcrop, its bulkheaded front and left side guarded by a narrow bunker and the splashing waters of the Caribbean. The 449-yard 6th is the most forgiving of the seaside holes – its immense fairway allowing plenty of room for safe shots, and even a preferred angle of approach from the drier right side.

The respite is only temporary, however. The 225-yard 7th is an all-carry proposition, requiring a long-iron across a wide curvature of water to a right-to-left angled green. In the course's early years – when it was selected to be among the first *World Atlas of Golf*'s best 18 holes worldwide – nearly all of this coastal area was covered by open sand, giving the 7th a slightly more rustic appearance than it enjoys today.

Finally, the 417-yard 8th follows the shoreline to a distinctive L-shaped green backed by a dangerous grass bunker. Hoping to inject a meaningful water carry into the drive, Dye created a peninsula tee by piling so many rocks in the surf that 'the natives thought I was building a causeway to Puerto Rico'.

THE BACK NINE

Though largely unheralded, the back nine's inland holes feature several appealing tests for the golfer, beginning with the 377-yard 10th, a dogleg left around a huge waste bunker that, particularly downwind, might well be carried. The 175-yard doughnut 13th is also memorable, for its green is an island set amid coral-lined sand and several overhanging trees.

The 505-yard lagoon-protected 14th runs close to the ocean, but play then returns to the coastline for real at the 384-yard 15th, a gentle dogleg right whose green is situated on a promontory, backed by sand and bulkheaded with coral. Playing into the prevailing wind, with its fairway flanked right by the sea and left by a surfeit of bunkers, this is certainly one of the game's most dangerous sub-400-yard par fours. The 185-yard 16th features more of the same – its left-to-right putting surface curving around a large bunker to a back corner again lined just above the waterline by coral.

The last of the coastal holes is the 435-yard 17th, a strong two-shotter made even tougher by both the prevailing breezes and the tendency to hit the tee shot out to the left side of a wide fairway, leaving a straight-on – but dangerously long – approach to the final waterside green. Generally overlooked after this spectacular oceanfront run is the 440-yard 18th, a snake-like double-dogleg with sand guarding the optimum right side of the fairway and a narrow green tucked away behind a wooded pond.

INTERNATIONAL GOLFING DESTINATION

Within four years of its opening in 1971, Teeth of the Dog had succeeded in making La Romana an international golfing destination of note. Its success spawned a second Dye layout known as the Links Course and, more recently, a 7,770-yard Dye-designed monster opened in 2004, giving the resort easily the largest and widest-ranging golf facilities in the Caribbean.

Once again the ocean threatens on the left of play at Teeth of the Dog.

Mid Ocean
Tuckers Town, Bermuda

Britain's oldest overseas territory, the 135 tiny islands that constitute Bermuda sit in scenic Atlantic Ocean splendour, some 650 miles south-east of Cape Hatteras, North Carolina. Blessed with a consistent sub-tropical climate, no fewer than eight golf courses fill its landmass of 22 square miles, led by the sublime Mid Ocean Golf Club.

Mid Ocean Golf Club
Tuckers Town, Bermuda

Designers: Charles Blair Macdonald and Seth Raynor, 1921

One man who in the years before commercial air travel recognized the tourist potential of Bermuda was Charles Blair Macdonald, a driving

CARD OF THE COURSE

HOLE	NAME	YARDS	PAR	HOLE	NAME	YARDS	PAR
1.	Atlantic	418	4	10.	Mercer Hill	404	4
2.	Long	471	5	11.	Trotts	487	5
3.	Eden	190	3	12.	Hillside	437	4
4.	Mangrove	330	4	13.	Biarritz	238	3
5.	Cape	433	4	14.	Leven	357	4
6.	Brow	360	4	15.	Punch Bowl	504	5
7.	Short	164	3	16.	LookOut	376	4
8.	Valley	349	4	17.	Redan	203	3
9.	Sound	406	4	18.	Home	421	4
OUT		3,121	35	IN		3,427	36
				TOTAL		6,548	71

During the 2007 PGA Grand Slam Angel Cabrera fell foul of the 1st hole's difficulties, running up an eight.

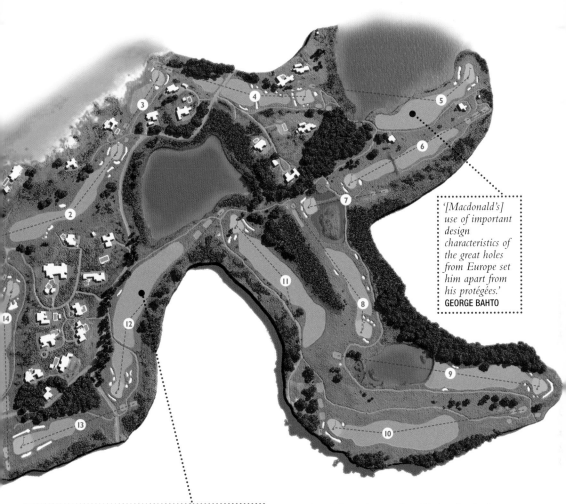

> '[Macdonald's] use of important design characteristics of the great holes from Europe set him apart from his protégées.'
> **GEORGE BAHTO**

> 'The contours of the property are unsurpassed, delightful valleys, one to two hundred yards in width, winding through coral hills from twenty to seventy-five feet in height, along the line of play'.
> **CHARLES BLAIR MACDONALD**

force behind golf's early American growth and designer of the seminal National Golf Links of America in 1911. Seeking a sunny retreat from the cold of the New York winter (not to mention a place where alcohol was legal in the brand-new era of Prohibition), Macdonald piggybacked onto the development interests of the Furness, Withy Steamship Company when he purchased the 600 Tuckers Town acres that would eventually become the Mid Ocean Golf Club.

The location, Macdonald believed, was perfect. Years later, he would observe that: 'One leaving New York about noon Saturday in the dead of winter can by ten o'clock Monday morning be teeing off in a summer climate and play over this wonderful, unexcelled course.'

THE MACDONALD/RAYNOR PARTNERSHIP

Thus motivated, the semiretired Macdonald became actively involved in Mid Ocean's design, walking the site with his talented partner Seth Raynor, and bringing in future architects Charles Banks (who would later build the well-known Castle Harbour Golf Club immediately next door) and Ralph Barton to aid in construction. With agronomic prospects vastly better in the property's lush valleys than on its coral-based hills, a routing was developed that stuck primarily to the lowlands. His plans so drawn, Macdonald left their construction to Raynor, Banks and Barton. On the course's 1921 completion, Macdonald proclaimed Mid Ocean to be 'an achievement in a semitropical climate as great as the National Golf Links of America has been in the temperate zone'.

Macdonald's characteristic immodesty notwithstanding, Mid Ocean certainly was a unique proposition for the tropics. Its rolling, highly scenic design easily exceeded anything in Britain's various warm-weather territories or, for that matter, any course yet built in Florida. Like all Macdonald/Raynor projects, it included several template holes borrowed from the great links of the Old World, though on this occasion these replicas were confined mostly to the par threes.

A CHALLENGING START

From a clubhouse situated on high ground, Mid Ocean begins with a difficult two-shotter played to a green perched on an oceanside cliff. This is also one's initial encounter with rows of tiny fairway bunkers, which are the residue of a 1953 Robert Trent Jones Snr visit during which nearly all of Raynor's larger hazards were inexplicably divided up.

A lost stroke might well be reclaimed at the short par-five 2nd before the golfer faces the first of the replica holes, the 190-yard Eden 3rd. Unlike the original 11th at St Andrews, Mid Ocean's 3rd features a rocky left-side plunge to the ocean rather than the eponymous estuary behind the green.

The 330-yard 4th, while not a replica, is decidedly Old World in style, crossing a quiet local road before requiring a blind pitch to a squarish, two-tiered green.

THE FAMED FIFTH

What follows, the 433-yard 5th, is not only Mid Ocean's best-known hole, but also one of the most recognized in all of golf. Conceptually modelled after Macdonald's original Cape hole – the 14th at the National Golf Links of America – the 5th wraps itself around the shoreline of Mangrove Lake, its angled fairway and steeply elevated tee providing both a remarkable view and an opportunity to bite off as much of the water carry as possible. Assuming that some part of the fairway is safely found, what remains is a fairly long approach to a platform green angled right-to-left above the shoreline, and flanked (particularly front-left) by deep, grassed-face bunkers.

Though less talked about, the 7th is a charming one-shotter at least somewhat based on another Macdonald original at the National Golf Links – the bunker-ringed Short. Here a nice variation is provided by a small pond that replaces sand in front and to the sides of the green, an enhanced difficulty at least partially offset by both the absence of the traditional horseshoe-shaped ridge within the putting surface and the fact that the hole plays noticeably downhill.

While the blind approach on the 406-yard 9th represents something of an Alps rendition, the strongest remaining par four is the 437-yard 12th. This is the longest of the two-shotters and one requiring a demanding uphill second shot to a pitched green whose entrance is narrowed by seven small bunkers.

REPLICAS OF NOTE

Both of the back-nine par threes are replicas, one following its template exactly while the other adds something of a new wrinkle. The more predictable is the 13th, a rendition of a perennial Macdonald/Raynor favourite, the Biarritz. This requires a long approach to a squarish green flanked on either side by geometric bunkering and with a narrow, deep swale in front. Except for its elevated tee, Mid Ocean's version is indistinguishable from numerous others, but with a long-iron or wooden club in hand par is always a good score.

Following the return of the uphill par-four 16th to the clubhouse, the 203-yard 17th differs somewhat from a traditional Redan, plunging substantially downhill in direct contrast to North Berwick's flattish, semiblind original. Like so many Macdonald/Raynor Redans, however, its challenge lies in choosing the proper line of approach to a fall-away green angled right-to-left behind a cluster of bunkers – the Trent Jones-divided

remains of a larger, more frightening hazard that originally existed here.

The 421-yard 18th begins with a tee placed seductively above a secluded beach and, though routed parallel to the ocean, is actually situated far enough from the cliff that only a prodigious slice will bring the water into play. Though a strong par four since its inception, the hole today features an alternate bluff-top tee measuring 521 yards, from which it becomes an excitingly reachable par five.

SOURCE OF PROSPERITY

While Macdonald's observation that prior to his arrival 'there was no golf course in Bermuda worthy of the name' may have been true, the construction of Mid Ocean quickly sparked a golfing boom on the island. Indeed, courses soon popped up at Riddell's Bay, the Belmont Hotel and Castle Harbour, and today this tiny territory with its six regulation and two short courses is among the most dense golfing destinations on Earth.

The unusual 15th hole unfolds towards a punchbowl green hidden behind a fifteen-foot hillock.

Index

Picture credits

Alamy All Canada Photos 174; Brian Morgan 116; Craig Lovell/Eagle Visions Photography 165; FPI 135; LA/AeroPhotos 133; M Timothy O'Keefe 201; ZUMA Press 91
Ballyhack Golf Club 60
Ballyneal Golf Club @Dick Durrance 2013 118
Bandon Dunes Golf Resort photo Wood Sabold 136
Cabot Links 173
Chris Gallow Photography 190
Clive Barber 186, 183, 188
Corbis Bettmann 8; Don Feria 156; Tony Roberts 16, 50, 94, 102, 141, 146, 154, 160, 164, 194
Courtesy **Fairmont Hotels & Resorts** for Banff Springs Golf Course 6, 178, 179
Four Seasons Hotels and Resorts, Costa Rica 1, 197
Getty Images David Alexander 73, 99, 107, 110; David Cannon 11, 47, 54, 114, 124, 128; Fred Vulch 35, 39, 82; Greg Vaughn 137; Jonathan Daniel 95; Lou Capozzola 22; Montana Pritchard/PGA of America 92; Phil Sheldon 10, 59, 64; Andy Lyons 103
www.golfclubatlas.com 26, 46, 69, 169
The Golf Picture Library Aidan Bradley 200; Evan Schiller 19, 86, 134; Larry Lambrecht 23, 31, 90; Matthew Harris 144
Courtesy of **The Greenbrier** 62
Courtesy **Kohler Co** for Whistling Straits 4, 115
Lambrecht Photography L C Lambrecht 2, 17, 27, 42, 43, 96, 97, 119, 132
Mahogany Run Golf Course 196
Courtesy of **The Omni Homestead Resort** for the Cascades Course 68
Paa-Ko Ridge Golf Club photo Robert Reck 120
Pasatiempo Golf Club photo Rob Babcock 130
Photoshot Fotosports 63
www.pineneedles-midpines.com 65
Press Association Images AP/Eric Risberg 150; Mary Ann Chastain/AP 76
Royal Colwood Golf Club 172
Shutterstock Pierre E Debbas 34; Danny E Hooks 80
Sports Legends & World Heroes Hy Peskin 9
Visions in Golf Christer Hoglund 106

An Hachette UK Company
www.hachette.co.uk

First published in Great Britain in 2014
by Hamlyn, a division of Octopus Publishing Group Ltd
Endeavour House
189 Shaftesbury Avenue
London
WC2H 8JY
www.octopusbooks.co.uk
www.octopusbooksusa.com

Some of this material previously appeared in
The World Atlas of Golf: The Greatest Courses and How They Are Played

Copyright © Octopus Publishing Group Ltd 2014

Distributed in U.S. by Hachette Book Group USA, 237 Park Avenue, New York NY 10017 USA

Distributed in Canada by Canadian Manda Group, 165 Dufferin Street, Toronto, Ontario, Canada M6K 3HG

ISBN 978-0-600-62847-7

A CIP catalogue record for this book is available from the Library of Congress
Printed and bound in China
10 9 8 7 6 5 4 3 2 1

Every effort has been made to ensure that the course cards, illustrations and text in this book are as accurate as possible. However, golf courses are frequently being adjusted and redesigned. The publishers would be grateful for any information which will assist them in updating future editions.